Horses & Ponies

WRITTEN BY
Sandy Ransford

PHOTOGRAPHED BY
Bob Langrish

Kingfisher would like to thank
The Talland School of Equitation,
Gloucestershire, England,
for their invaluable help in
the production of this book.

KINGFISHER
Kingfisher Publications Plc
New Penderel House
283-288 High Holborn
London WC1V 7HZ

www.kingfisherpub.com

First published by
Kingfisher Publications Plc 2001
This paperback edition first published
by Kingfisher Publications Plc 2005
10 9 8 7 6 5 4 3 2 1

1TR/0105/TWP/CLSN/130ENSOMA

ISBN-13: 978 0 7534 1133 9
ISBN-10: 0 7534 1133 4

Designed and edited by
BOOKWORK
Editor: Louise Pritchard
Art Director: Jill Plank
Assistant Editor: Annabel Blackledge
Designer: Yolanda Carter

For Kingfisher:
Managing Editor: Miranda Smith
Managing Art Director: Mike Davis
DTP Manager: Nicky Studdart
Production Controllers: Jacquie
Horner, Caroline Hansell

Printed in Singapore

Contents

Presenting
horses
and ponies

Croup

Point of hip

Loins

Dock

Horses, ponies, wild asses and zebras all belong to the horse family. They are descended from the same ancestors but evolved differently. All domestic horses and ponies, from the biggest Shire horse to the tiniest miniature pony, are the same species. Ponies are smaller than horses, and often more mischievous.

Tail

Stifle

Flank

Thigh

Gaskin (second thigh)

Point of hock

Hock

Przewalski's wild horse
This species of wild horse was discovered in Mongolia in 1881. It looks very like the wild ancestors of modern domestic horses and ponies.

Points of a horse

It is useful to know the names and positions of all the 'points' of a horse or pony. It will help you to understand the instructions you are given when you learn to ride and look after a pony. The picture above shows the basic points – there are many more!

Tendons

Ergot (small lump on the back of the fetlock joint)

Heel

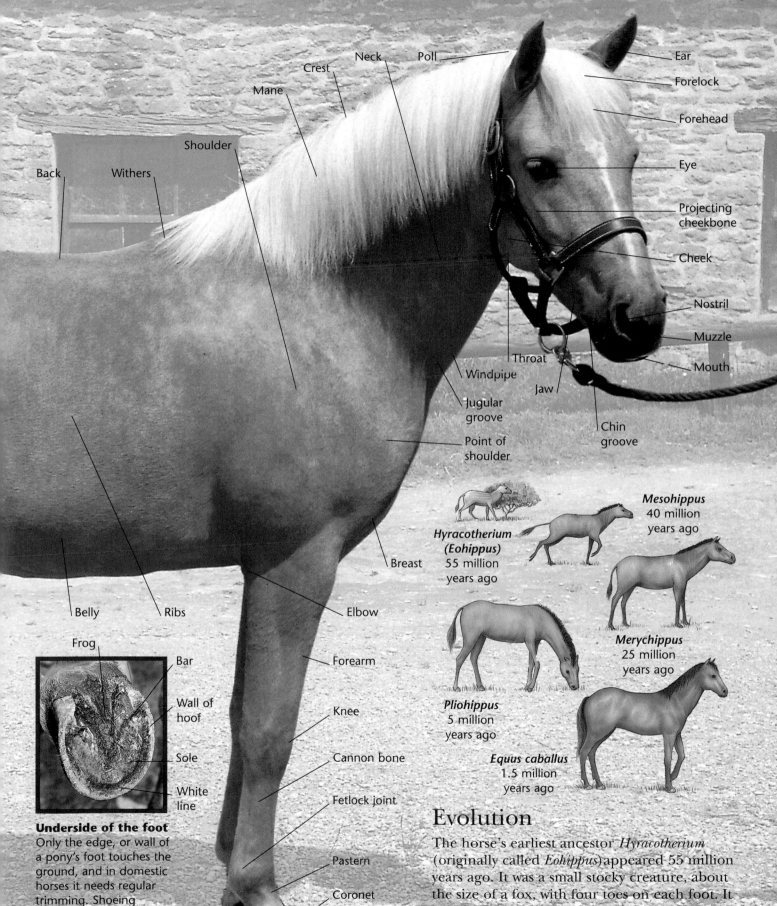

Back

Withers

Shoulder

Mane

Crest

Neck

Poll

Ear

Forelock

Forehead

Eye

Projecting cheekbone

Cheek

Nostril

Muzzle

Mouth

Throat

Windpipe

Jaw

Jugular groove

Chin groove

Point of shoulder

Breast

Belly

Ribs

Elbow

Forearm

Knee

Cannon bone

Fetlock joint

Pastern

Coronet

Wall of hoof

Frog

Bar

Wall of hoof

Sole

White line

Underside of the foot
Only the edge, or wall of a pony's foot touches the ground, and in domestic horses it needs regular trimming. Shoeing protects hooves from wearing away too fast.

Hyracotherium (Eohippus)
55 million years ago

Mesohippus
40 million years ago

Merychippus
25 million years ago

Pliohippus
5 million years ago

Equus caballus
1.5 million years ago

Evolution

The horse's earliest ancestor *Hyracotherium* (originally called *Eohippus*) appeared 55 million years ago. It was a small stocky creature, about the size of a fox, with four toes on each foot. It took several stages of evolution for the animal we know today (*Equus caballus*) to develop.

Natural world of horses

Horses and ponies are herd animals. They form small groups, and within the groups, there are particular friendships and sometimes dislikes. In the wild, horses spend up to 20 hours a day grazing, constantly moving slowly to find food. When they rest, at least one group member stands guard over their sleeping companions.

Domesticated horses

A pony can feel unhappy if he is kept on his own. If there are no other horses or ponies around, other animals, like sheep and cows, make quite good company. The life of a domesticated pony is not natural, so try to give your pony as much freedom as possible.

Mutual grooming

Wild and domesticated ponies often groom each other if they are friends. They scratch each other's neck, withers or back with their front teeth. This is their way of strengthening a friendship.

Flehmen reaction

A pony may curl up his top lip when he senses an unusual smell or taste. This curious action lets him draw air over a special sense organ in the roof of his mouth so that he can analyse the smell.

A horse's body language

Ears pricked forwards show that a horse is interested in what is going on, and expects good things to happen.

One ear to the side shows that the pony is distracted by something other than his main object of interest.

Ears laid back show anger or fear. The pony is warning you, or another pony, that he may kick or bite.

Herd animals

In the wild, horses and ponies, such as these mustangs in the USA, live in small family groups. These consist of one stallion, a few mares and their foals, and young animals that stay until they form herds of their own.

Fighting talk

In a group of horses and ponies, each animal has a position in a hierarchy, and squabbles occur if one horse tries to challenge for a higher position. In the wild, stallions fight off rivals, biting and striking out with a foreleg, or swinging their quarters round ready to kick. But horses and ponies threaten each other much more than they actually fight. Ears laid back and an outstretched neck are often enough to see off another pony.

Colours and markings

There are many variations in the colours of horses and ponies, but most are a shade of brown or grey, and have dark skins. Some horses and ponies change colour as they grow older. Most 'white' ponies were originally grey, but have become paler in colour with age. Completely black horses are rare.

Colours

Even within the colour groups there are different shades. Bays can be lighter or darker; greys vary from almost black to white. A pony's coat is described as white only if it has pink skin.

Dapple grey
Grey and black hairs forming clear rings

Piebald
Black and white areas all over the body

Palomino
Golden with a pale, often white, mane and tail

Brown
Dark brown with black mane, tail and legs

Chestnut
Red-gold all over with a similar mane and tail

Bay mare and foal
This mare with her foal is a bay. She has a rich brown coat and black 'points' – mane, tail and lower legs.

Star and stripe
This pony is bright chestnut. He has a white star and stripe on his face, and two white socks.

Appaloosa

The Appaloosa is an American breed of spotted horse. It has either a white coat with dark spots, or a dark coat spotted with white. Not all spotted horses are Appaloosas, but they may be described as being appaloosa colour.

Head markings

Horses and ponies often have white markings on their faces. A mark down the face is called a stripe. A broad stripe is often called a blaze. Some ponies have white faces.

White face　　　Stripe

Leg markings

A white band above the hoof is called a white coronet. A white pastern or fetlock is often called a sock. A white area reaching up the cannon to the knee or hock is called a white stocking.

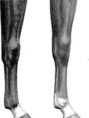

White coronet　White pastern　White fetlock　White cannon

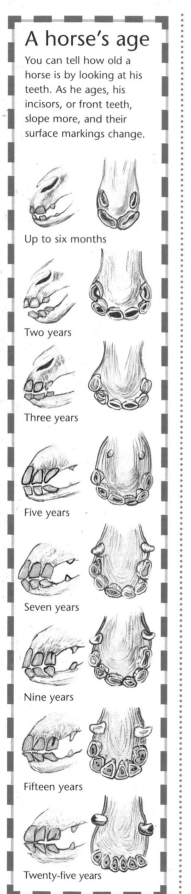
Learning more about horses

The more you get to know about horses and ponies, the more you will realize how much there is to learn. And if you keep a pony of your own, you owe it to him to learn as much as you can. When you know how a healthy horse or pony should look and behave, you will be able to notice any sign of ill health or lameness in your own pony.

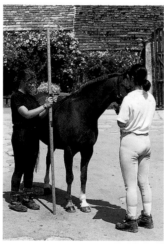

Measuring up

A horse is measured from the top of his withers to the ground. You can use a measuring stick with a horizontal bar that rests on the withers to give an accurate reading. Traditionally, horses and ponies are measured in 'hands'. There are 10 cm in a hand – about the width of an adult's hand. Today, height is also given in centimetres.

What is normal for your pony?

Although the general signs for good and bad health are the same for all horses and ponies, some may behave slightly differently. For example, it may seem odd for a pony to be lying down in the daytime, but some ponies like to have a nap around mid-morning. Get to know what is normal for your pony.

Senses

Like you, horses and ponies have five senses, but theirs are much more acute than yours. Your pony's wild ancestors were preyed on by wolves and other carnivores. Their finely tuned senses protected them in the wild by warning them when danger was near.

Sight
A horse's prominent eyes allow him to see behind, to the side and in front.

Smell and taste
His sense of smell is especially acute. He can even smell if a stranger is approaching.

Hearing
A horse's ears are very mobile – he can turn them in the direction of a sound quickly.

Touch
If a fly lands on a horse's skin, he is able to twitch the exact muscle to make it move.

Fit for anything

A healthy pony is alert and interested in everything that is going on around him. He has bright, clear eyes. Neither his eyes nor his nose are runny. His coat is shiny, and he always shows great interest in his food.

Horse breeds

For thousands of years, people have bred horses for specific purposes – heavy 'draught' ones for pulling a plough, hardy ones for herding cattle, or fast ones for racing. Now that people no longer use horses as their chief means of transport, they breed them for sport or competition. New breeds are still being created, as needs and demands change.

Palomino
In the USA, Palominos are a special breed. This Quarter Horse could be registered with both the Quarter Horse Association and the American Palomino Horse Association.

Arab
The oldest horse breed, the Arab is famed for its smooth action and stamina.

Lipizzaner
This strong horse is best known for its use by the Spanish Riding School.

Thoroughbred
Descended from the Arab, this is the fastest horse, and is used for racing.

Percheron
This heavy draught horse from France is grey or black. Unlike other heavy breeds it has no long hair or 'feather' on its legs.

Andalucian
Descended from the Spanish Horse, and the Barb from northern Africa, the Andalucian is usually bay or grey with a long wavy mane and tail. Although not a fast horse, it has excellent paces. Andalucians are now bred mainly in southern Spain.

Quarter Horse

The Quarter Horse is the first all-American breed. It got its name because it was bred to run in quarter-mile (400m) races. It is fast, nimble and has a calm temperament, and is therefore ideal for working with cattle.

Australian Stock Horse

The Australian Stock Horse was bred for work on Australia's cattle and sheep stations. It was developed in the 19th century from the Thoroughbred and the Waler. Easy to handle, it is a good all-round horse with great stamina.

❶ Selle Francais

This French horse was bred for showjumping, and also does well in eventing.

❷ Waler

This name is a short form of New South Wales in Australia. The horse excels at jumping.

❸ Akhal-Teke

From Turkmenistan, in northern Asia, this breed is often a golden colour.

❹ Saddlebred

This breed from the USA has special gaits, or paces. It can be three- or five-gaited.

❺ Morgan

Morgans are descended from the American stallion Justin Morgan, born in the 1790s.

❻ Standardbred

The Standardbred is an American harness-racing horse. Some horses race at a trot, but others 'pace', i.e. they move their legs on the same side together, instead of moving diagonally.

❼ Trakehner

A tall Eastern European horse, the Trakehner is excellent at jumping and dressage.

Pony breeds

A pony is not more than 147cm (14.2h) high. There are many different breeds of pony in the world. Some, like the native breeds of Britain, have existed for thousands of years in a semi-wild state. Others, like the American Shetland, have been specially developed by people in the last 100 years. Most of the ponies you meet will not be pure-bred.

Icelandic Pony
Descended from Norwegian and Scottish island ponies, the Icelandic pony has existed for more than 1,000 years and was once Iceland's chief means of transport. Although it is small – 122–132cm (12–13h) – it is usually called a horse, and is strong and hardy.

Welsh Pony
There are four breeds of Welsh pony ranging from the largest, the Welsh Cob, to the smallest, the Welsh Mountain Pony. In between are the Welsh Pony and the Welsh Pony of Cob Type. This mare with her foal is a Welsh Mountain Pony.

Australian Pony

Recognized as a breed since the 1920s, the Australian Pony was developed from several imported breeds, notably the Welsh Mountain Pony, which it resembles. Well proportioned, with good action and temperament, it is a quality riding pony.

Chincoteague

Chincoteague and Assateague ponies are some of the last truly wild ponies in the world. They live on islands off the coast of Virginia, USA, and may be the descendants of Barb horses from North Africa that were shipwrecked there in the 16th century.

American Shetland

Bred in the 20th century, largely from Hackney Ponies, the American Shetland has a narrow build. It is a popular harness pony in the USA.

❶ Highland
The Highland from Scotland is often grey or dun. It is a popular trekking pony.

❷ Dales
Black, bay or brown, the Dales is a driving pony originally from northern England.

❸ New Forest Pony
The New Forest Pony is a popular riding pony that originates from southern England.

❹ Connemara
The only native Irish pony, the Connemara is a good all-rounder. It is often grey.

❺ Fjord
Cream or dun in colour, with a dark dorsal stripe, the Fjord comes from Norway.

❻ Fell
Always black or brown, the Fell can be ridden or driven, and comes from northern England.

❼ Dartmoor
An excellent riding pony from southwest England, the Dartmoor is a good jumper.

❽ Haflinger
Chestnut or palomino, the Haflinger is a strong riding or driving pony from Austria.

❾ Shetland
Stocky and extremely strong, this tiny pony is from the Shetland Islands, off Scotland.

❿ Caspian
The Caspian comes from the Arabian peninsula. It is fast, and a skilful jumper.

Bridles and other tack

T ack is the name for the equipment that you use on a horse or pony, including bridle and bit, saddle, girth, stirrups and martingale. A bridle's name – e.g. snaffle or double – refers to its bit. Ponies usually wear a snaffle bridle. Bridles are made in different sizes and you can buy parts separately. Each bit design works in a slightly different way and suits different horses and ponies.

Snaffle bridle

Western bridle
This Western bridle has a split headpiece that fits around the ears. The reins are not fastened together and are held in one hand. Some Western bridles are bitless, but others have a long-cheeked curb bit.

Western tack

Western tack is similar to that used by cowboys, whose horses were trained to respond to the slightest touch on the reins. To stop their saddles from slipping, the horses wore breastplates. These attached to the saddle and were held in place by straps over the withers.

Running martingale

Standing martingale

Martingales

A martingale is designed to stop a horse or pony from throwing up his head. It consists of a long strap, which fastens round the girth at one end. The other end of a standing martingale buckles round the noseband. A running martingale divides into two straps ending in rings, through which the reins pass. Both kinds of martingale are held in place by a neck-strap.

Snaffle bridle

The simplest bridle is called a snaffle bridle. It can be fitted with different nosebands and bits. The cavesson noseband and snaffle bit are used the most often.

Headpiece

Browband

Cavesson noseband

Cheekpiece

Throatlash

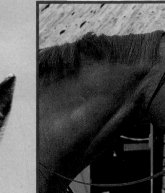

Double bridle

This bridle has two bits – a snaffle called a bridoon, and a curb bit called a Weymouth. A curb bit has long cheeks. It is used with a curb chain and lip-strap.

Eggbutt snaffle

Loose-ring snaffle

Mullen-mouth snaffle

French-link snaffle

Kimblewick curb bit

Pelham curb bit

Flash noseband

Eggbutt snaffle bit

Reins

Bits

An eggbutt snaffle is designed to stop the rings pinching the corners of a horse's mouth. Pelhams and Kimblewicks are types of curb bit. The curb chain rests in the groove of the horse's chin. When pressure is put on the reins, the chain tightens, giving the rider more control.

Flash noseband
Named after a horse called Flash that wore one, this kind of noseband is attached to the front of a cavesson. It fastens under the bit and helps to keep a horse or pony's mouth shut.

Girths

The saddle is held in place by a girth, which is buckled on to the girth straps under the saddle flap. Girths are made of leather, webbing or synthetic material. Some, such as a Balding girth, are specially shaped to avoid rubbing the pony's elbows.

Leather Balding girth

Foam-padded synthetic girth

Webbing girth

Types of saddle

Saddles are made on a rigid framework called a tree, which is made of wood and metal, or sometimes fibreglass. Traditionally the seat is made of pigskin, although sometimes other leathers are used. Nowadays, some saddles are made from synthetic materials, which are cheaper. There are several kinds of saddle, shaped according to their intended use – general riding, jumping, dressage or showing.

Saddle flap

Knee roll

Buckle guard

Girth straps

Sweat flap

The basic saddle

A general purpose saddle is suitable for most types of riding. It has forward-cut flaps and slight knee rolls to prevent your knees from sliding forwards when jumping. You can use this kind of saddle equally well for riding out, for a showing class at a local show and for dressage at riding-club level.

Gullet

Pommel

Seat

Cantle

Lining over panel

Waist

Skirt

D-ring

Surcingle loop

Knee roll

Saddle flap

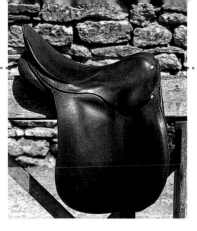

Dressage saddle

The dressage saddle is designed to help you to sit deep in the seat with a long leg position. Like the show saddle, which is shaped to show off the horse's shoulders, it has straight flaps.

Cleaning tack

You should clean your tack every time you use it. Clean, supple leather will not crack, break or rub the pony. When you clean it, check the stitching to make sure that nothing needs repairing.

First, wash the bit. Clean the grease and dirt off the bridle, saddle and stirrup leathers with a damp cloth, then rub with saddle soap all over, working it in well. Do not get the sponge too wet because water is bad for the leather.

Cleaning the bridle on a hanging hook

Cleaning the saddle on a saddle horse

Knee rolls
Large knee rolls support your knee comfortably when you take up a jumping position.

Showjumping saddle

The showjumping saddle is designed for use with shorter stirrup leathers. It is shaped to help you to sit correctly in a forward position and maintain balance. It has pronounced forward-cut flaps, large knee rolls, and may have a deep seat.

Western saddle

The Western saddle was originally designed for cowboys, who tied roped steers to the high horn at the front. It has wooden stirrups, which are comfortable for the feet. In his heyday, the cowboy lived in his saddle. He spent hours riding, and the saddle carried all he needed.

Side-saddle

For 600 years, up until the early 20th century, women rode side-saddle. Today, you usually see side-saddle riding only in the show ring. The rider's legs fit around two pommels. She controls the near side of the horse with her left leg, and the off side with a long whip.

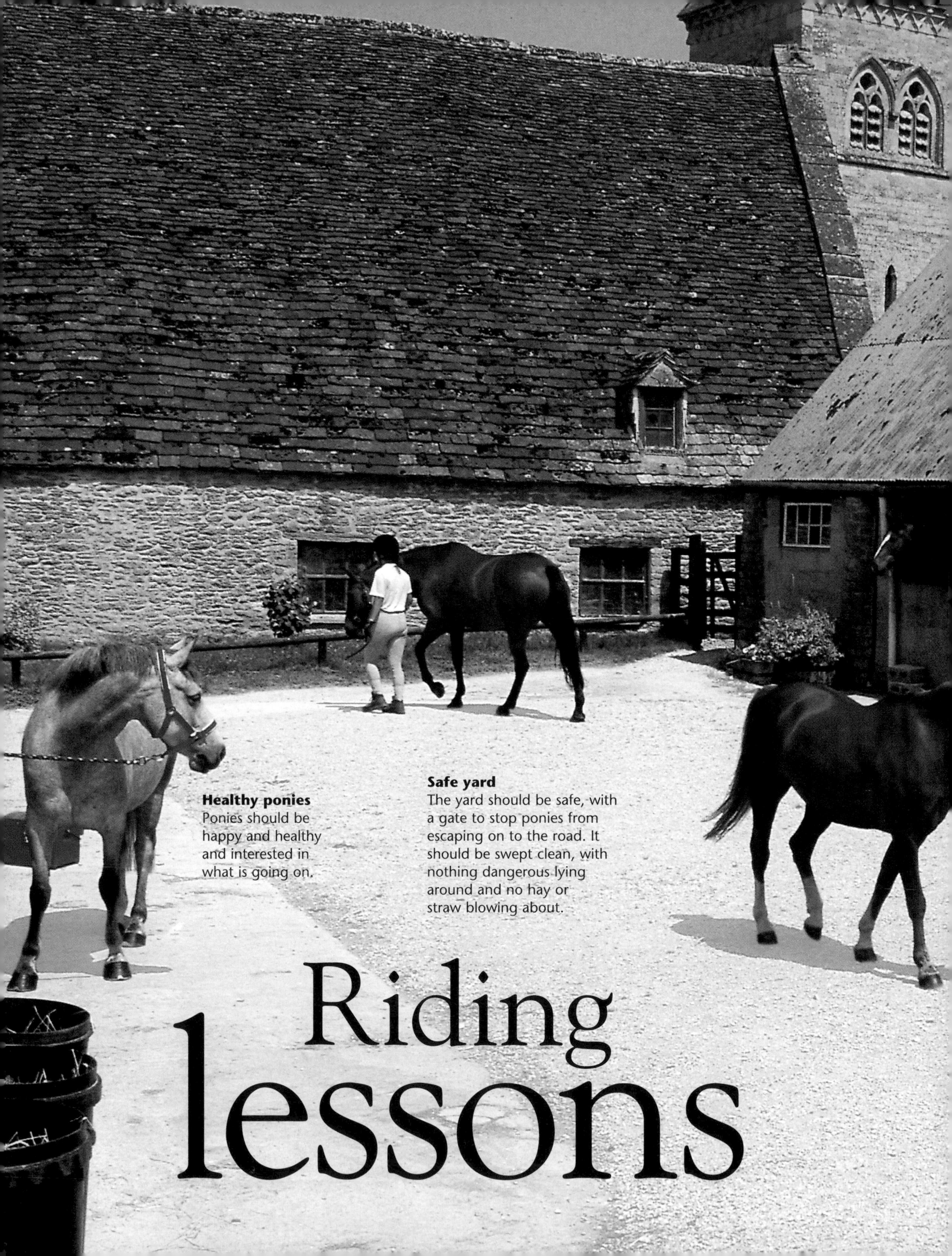

Healthy ponies
Ponies should be
happy and healthy
and interested in
what is going on.

Safe yard
The yard should be safe, with
a gate to stop ponies from
escaping on to the road. It
should be swept clean, with
nothing dangerous lying
around and no hay or
straw blowing about.

Riding
lessons

Tidy tack room
For the safety of riders, and comfort of ponies, tack must be looked after properly. It should be stored neatly.

Knowledgeable staff
The staff and helpers should know how to handle the horses and ponies safely and quietly. They should be friendly and helpful.

Happy clients
Look out for other children learning to ride and enjoying themselves.

When you decide to learn to ride, it is important to choose a good riding centre. If possible, visit more than one before you book a lesson. Have a good look round and find out if there is a proper school in which to have lessons. The horses and ponies should look well-fed, clean and contented. All the stables should be clean, and the yard and tack room tidy.

Riding clothes

Hunting
cap

Tie

Hacking
jacket

Riding wear used to be very formal, but today you can wear much more casual clothes. The one essential is a hard hat. This can be a skull cap, which is usually covered with a silk, or a velvet-covered hunting cap. You can wear heeled shoes for riding, but jodhpur (ankle-length) or riding (knee-length) boots are safer and more comfortable. You will also find stretchy jodhpurs more comfortable than ordinary trousers.

Looking the part

Whether you wear formal or casual clothes when you are on your pony, you should always try to look neat and tidy. Tuck in your shirt, and if you have long hair, tie it back or wear a hair net.

Non-slip
gloves

Cool
cotton
shirt

Stretch
jodhpurs

Riding
boots

Jodhpur
boots

Smart
Formal wear is usually necessary for dressage and showjumping events.

Casual
Without a tie and jacket, you will feel more comfortable when having lessons or riding for fun.

Stay warm

In wet weather, a full-length macintosh will keep you dry. Special straps will stop it blowing off your legs. Gloves will stop the reins slipping out of your hands.

In cold weather, wear leggings under jodhpurs.

Wet weather gear

Western dress

Classic Western dress is like the costumes worn by cowboys in the films – a broad-brimmed hat tied with a cord, a colourful shirt and neckerchief, jeans, chaps (leg covers, usually made from leather) and high-heeled boots. Today, young riders wear hard hats for safety, and may go without chaps in warm weather.

Skull cap with coloured silk

Matching sweatshirt

Body protector

Whip

Half chaps

Formal clothes

For showing classes, you will look smartest in a black jacket, hat and boots with light-coloured jodhpurs. Find out what you need to wear before you go to a show. You may be able to wear jodhpur boots or long riding boots.

Clothes for jumping

You should always wear a body protector for jumping. It will help to protect you from back injuries if you fall off. For showjumping you should wear a formal jacket on top, but you can look more casual for cross-country. It is fun to wear matching 'colours'.

First meeting

Getting close to a horse or pony for the first time can be a bit alarming, but there is nothing to be afraid of. Most ponies are very gentle. Move slowly and quietly and do not shout or wave your arms about. Meeting a new pony is a bit like meeting a stranger. If you walk up confidently and talk in a friendly way, the pony will immediately feel at ease.

Introducing yourself

Approach a pony from the front and slightly from the side, walking towards his head so he can get a good look at you. Talk to him so that he can hear you and knows you are a friend. When you get close, let him smell your hand, then pat him on the neck and show him that you are not frightened of him.

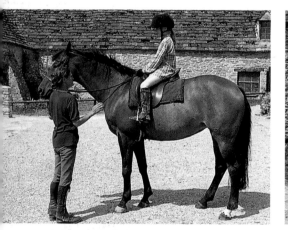

Horse too large
This horse is too large for the rider. The girl's lower legs are in contact with the saddle flaps instead of the horse's sides.

Pony too small
This pony is too small for the rider. The girl's legs are not in contact with the pony, and she may be too heavy for it.

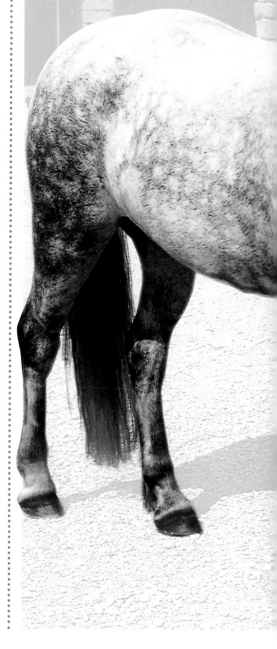

The right size

A riding school will give you a pony to ride that is the right size for you. When you are sitting correctly in the saddle, the soles of your feet should be level with the line of the pony's belly. You will then be able to use your legs in the right place, just behind the pony's girth.

Handling ponies

Walk, do not run around the stable-yard and paddocks when ponies are about. Do not get cross or flustered.

Speak quietly to ponies and to friends. Do not shout, or shriek with laughter.

Walk up to a pony confidently. Do not be nervous or you will make him nervous.

Give a pony a pat, or stroke his neck quite firmly so as not to tickle him.

Talk to ponies in a firm, friendly way, as if you are used to telling them what to do.

Offer a titbit such as a piece of carrot or apple or special pony treat. Food helps in almost any situation!

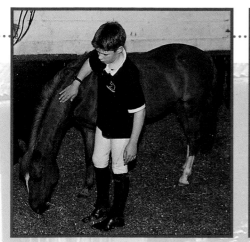

In the stable

Always let your pony know where you are, so you do not startle him. If you have to walk round his rear end, put a hand on his quarters and slide it down his tail as you go round. This will stop him from moving backwards.

Offering food
Hold your hand out flat with the food on it. Keep your thumb out of the way so that the pony does not bite it by mistake.

Making friends
Listen to what the instructor tells you and do what she says. You will soon make friends with the pony.

Put on the noseband
Standing on the pony's left, or near, side, put your right arm under his chin and slip on the noseband.

Getting ready

There is a lot to do before you can get on a pony and ride. When you have got used to handling ponies, you may have to go out to the field and catch yours before leading him back to the stable. Then you can give him a good grooming. When the pony is clean and ready, you will have to tack him up – that is, put on his saddle and bridle. Always give your pony plenty of time to digest his food before you ride him.

Buckle up
Gently flick the headpiece over the pony's head with your right hand. Hold the cheekpiece in your left hand then reach for the headpiece with your right hand and fasten the buckle.

Putting on a headcollar

You will use a headcollar to lead a pony from place to place and to tie him up. Most ponies do not mind having a headcollar put on, but if you have to catch one that is difficult, it may help if you hold out a titbit while you put on the noseband.

Leading a pony

It is traditional to lead a pony on the left-hand side. This is called the near side. (The other side is called the off side.) Hold the rope with your right hand near the pony's head and your left hand near the end of the rope.

Holding the rope like this means that, if the pony misbehaves, you can let go with your right hand while keeping hold with the left, and he will simply go round you in a circle.

When you lead a pony, walk at his shoulder and look where you are going. Do not keep looking back at the pony and do not pull him along. When you want to turn, walk round the pony.

Tying up

Tie the lead rope to a piece of string which will break easily if the pony is startled and pulls back. If the pony cannot break free, he may panic even more and hurt himself. Tie the rope with a quick-release knot. You can undo this quickly in an emergency by pulling the loose end.

1 Put on the numnah or saddle cloth – the pad that goes under the saddle. Place it a little too far forwards to begin with.

Putting on a saddle

The saddle should sit just behind the pony's withers. The girth goes about one hand's width behind the pony's elbow. You should learn how to put on a saddle even if your pony is usually tacked up when you arrive at the riding school. It is fun to do it yourself, and the more you are able to do for a pony, the better you will get to know him.

2 Lower the saddle on to the numnah. Hold the numnah up into the gullet of the saddle, with your left hand on the pommel and your right on the cantle. Slide the saddle and numnah back into position.

3 If there are loops on the numnah, slip a girth strap through on both sides. This will stop it from slipping.

4 Attach the girth on the off side, then let it hang down. Bring it under the pony's belly from the near side.

5 Use the front two girth straps, or the front and back straps. Do up the girth loosely until you are ready to go.

Putting on a bridle

Stand on a pony's left side to put on a bridle. If she will not take the bit, wiggle your thumb in the corner of her mouth and press gently on the gum in the gap between her teeth.

1 Take off the headcollar and re-fasten it round the pony's neck so she cannot walk away from you.

2 Put the reins over her head with your right hand. Hold the bridle in your left hand while you do so.

3 Slip your right arm under the pony's jaw to hold the bridle in front of her face. Press the bit into her mouth with your left hand.

All tacked up

When you have saddled the pony, you can put on her bridle. Many ponies dislike their girths being fastened, and blow themselves out to stop you. Tacking up in this order gives the pony time to forget about her girth, making it easier for you to tighten it before mounting. Hold up the bridle to check no part of it is twisted before you put it on.

Leaving a pony tacked up

If you need to leave your pony tacked up, twist the reins round each other and fasten the throatlash through them. This stops them from going over the pony's head. To tie her up, put on a headcollar over the bridle. Leave the girth loose and do not pull down the stirrups until you are ready to mount.

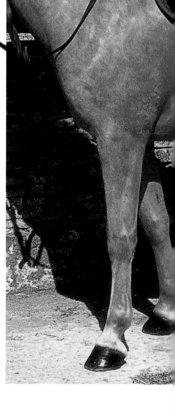

4 Fold down the pony's ears and pass the headpiece over them. Pull out the forelock over the browband.

5 Do up the throatlash. You should be able to fit your fist between it and the pony when it is fastened.

6 Now fasten the noseband. Make sure that you can fit two fingers underneath it when it is done up.

7 If the bridle has a flash noseband, fasten this last. Buckle it round the pony's nose below the bit.

Ready to go

Before mounting, always make a habit of checking the tack. See that the bridle is on correctly, that all the straps are fastened and the ends put through their keepers. Check that the girth is not twisted and that it is fastened on the correct straps. Last of all, make sure that the girth is tight enough.

Taking tack off

Tie up your pony before removing the tack. Put the headcollar round her neck while you take off the bridle. Do not leave the saddle on with the girth undone – it could fall off and get damaged.

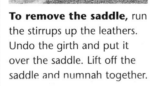

To remove the saddle, run the stirrups up the leathers. Undo the girth and put it over the saddle. Lift off the saddle and numnah together.

To remove the bridle, undo the throatlash and noseband. Slip the bridle over the head.

Carrying the bridle over your shoulder prevents the reins from dangling on the floor.

Carry a saddle on your forearm, with the pommel at your elbow and the girth over the seat. Carry the bridle over the same shoulder. This leaves you with one hand free to open a door or turn on a light when necessary.

Mounting and dismounting

Before you can learn to ride, you have to know how to get on and off a pony safely. Even if you use a mounting block in the school, there will be times when you are out riding when you have to dismount to open a gate. You can check if the stirrup leathers are roughly the right length for you before you first get on your pony. Put the tips of your fingers on the stirrup bar and stretch out the leather and iron along your arm. The iron should just reach into your armpit.

Getting a leg up

This is an easy way to mount. Hold the reins in your left hand and put your right hand on the saddle. Bend your left knee so your helper can hold your leg. On the count of three, spring off the ground, and your helper will lift you up at the same time.

1 Holding the reins in your left hand, put your left foot carefully in the stirrup.

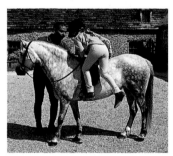

2 Hold the saddle with your right hand and spring up off the ground. Do not pull yourself up.

3 Swing your right leg over the pony's quarters, being careful not to kick her.

4 Lower yourself gently into the saddle and put your right foot in the stirrup.

Mounting

When you first learn to mount a pony, it is helpful if someone holds it still for you. Make a habit of always checking that the girth is tight enough before you start, or the saddle will slip round. If you do not have a helper, and your pony is inclined to wander off, stand her facing a gate or a wall so that she cannot move forwards.

Alternative dismounting

In some countries, you may be taught to dismount by reversing the mounting process. Take your right foot out of the stirrup, but keep your left foot in the stirrup. Swing your right leg over the pony's quarters and step down, landing on the right foot first. Finally, take your left foot out of the stirrup.

Dismounting

Take both feet out of the stirrups. Hold the reins in your left hand, put your hand on the pony's neck and lean forwards slightly. Put your right hand on the saddle, then swing your right leg over the pony's quarters. Slip to the ground gently, bending your knees as you land. Keep clear of the pony's feet.

Sitting correctly

Sitting correctly in the saddle puts you in the best position to give the aids – the signals by which you tell your pony what to do. This position also looks good, but try not to concentrate so hard that you stiffen up. You need to stay supple and relaxed so that your whole body goes with the movement of your pony. Riding will then be comfortable for both of you.

Stirrup length

You can check if your stirrups are the right length by sitting in the saddle with your legs hanging down. If the tread of the iron is level with your ankle, the stirrups are about right.

Adjusting your stirrups

Hold the reins in one hand and adjust the stirrup with the other. Pull up the end of the leather, keeping your foot in the stirrup. When the prong is in the hole, pull down the underneath part of the leather so the buckle is at the top.

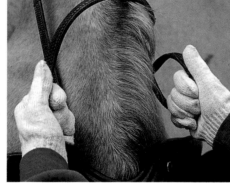

Holding the reins

Single reins go between your little and ring fingers and up through your hands. Hold the reins with your thumbs on top. You should be able to feel your pony's mouth all the time. This is called 'the contact'. As you ride, allow your hands to move with the pony's head.

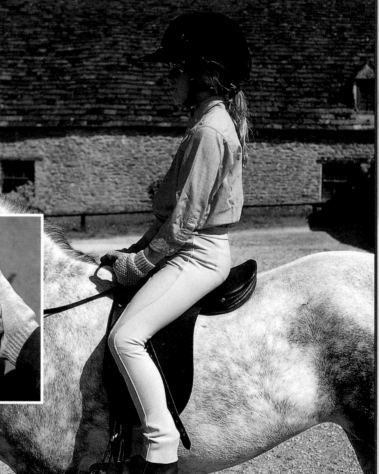

Straight line

When you are sitting in the saddle, try to imagine there is a line going straight down through your ear, shoulder, hip and heel.

Sitting in the saddle

Keep your heels down and your toes pointing forwards, with the balls of your feet resting on the stirrup irons. Your lower legs should be behind the girth and your back should be straight. Hold your arms by your sides, and your forearms in line with the reins leading to your pony's mouth.

Sit up straight

Look up and ahead of you

Relax your shoulders and elbows to allow your hands to move with the pony's mouth

Let your seat, thighs and knees lie relaxed on the saddle

Do not bend your wrists, but keep them relaxed.

Rest your lower legs against the pony's sides

Keep your heels down

In balance
Sit square in the lowest part of the saddle. Your weight should be balanced equally on each side.

Checking the girth

To test whether the girth is tight enough, lean forwards and push two fingers under it. If there is just room for your fingers, it is all right. If there is room for more fingers, the girth needs tightening.

Keep hold of the reins with your right hand

To tighten the girth, move your leg forwards and lift the saddle flap. Pull upwards on the girth strap and guide the buckle's prong into a higher hole with your finger.

Halt to walk

Sit up straight and 'feel' the pony's mouth through the reins. Press her sides with the calves of your legs and say "Walk on." When the pony obeys, relax the reins a little, but stay in contact with her mouth.

Walking on

The walk is a horse or pony's slowest pace. It has four beats, with each foot hitting the ground separately. The sequence is right hind, right fore, left hind, left fore, but there are always two feet on the ground. As a horse walks, she nods her head slightly, and you should let your hands follow this movement. Walking allows you the time to concentrate on your position, and apply the aids correctly.

Standing still
The aim when halting is to get your pony to stand in a balanced position. She should be ready to go forward again when you ask.

Walk to halt

Sit down deep in the saddle and press the calves of your legs against the pony's sides to 'ride her forwards' into the halt. Keep firm pressure on the reins, but do not pull roughly. As soon as the pony responds, relax the pressure.

The walk

A pony should take even, regular steps, and walk forwards energetically. Her hindfeet may leave prints on the ground in front of those left by her forefeet. This is called overtracking.

Natural aids

Your legs drive a pony forwards, creating the energy she needs for each movement.

Your hands control the energy created, and guide the movements.

Your seat drives the pony forwards, and shifts of weight give instructions.

Your voice can give encouragement, slow her down, or tell her off if she does not do what you want.

Turning left

Inside leg lies near the girth

Outside leg lies behind the girth

Western style

To ride Western style, you sit with your legs almost straight, holding the reins in one hand. You turn by pressing the rein against your pony's neck, or 'neck-reining', on the opposite side to where you want to go.

Turning left or right

To turn left, keep your left leg (the leg on the inside of the turn) near the girth. Draw your right (outside) leg back behind the girth and press it against the pony's side. Pull slightly with the left rein, resting the right rein against the pony's neck and looking in the direction of the turn. Reverse these aids to turn right.

Turning right

Asking a pony to trot

The trot is called a two-beat pace because there are two beats to every stride. The pony's feet hit the ground in diagonal pairs – right fore and left hind together, then left fore and right hind together. The trot is a faster pace than walk. A change of pace is called a transition. Changing to a faster pace, such as from walk to trot, is an upward transition. Changing to a slower pace, such as from trot to walk, is a downward transition.

Learning to rise

The trot will feel bumpy for you when you are riding. To even out the bumps, you can rise to the trot. You lift yourself out of the saddle on one beat and sit in the saddle on the other. You can practise this in halt.

Trot on
As your pony goes into trot, allow your hands to go with the movement of her head.

Back to walk
When you want to walk, sit down in the saddle and keep a contact with your legs and hands.

Transitions

When you want to ask your pony to trot, shorten your reins, drive the pony on with your legs, then relax the rein a little to allow her to go forwards. To ask your pony to walk again, squeeze with your legs, but resist the forward movement with your hands.

Rising trot

When you are rising to the trot, lift yourself a little way out of the saddle, and then lower yourself gently. Try not to bump about.

Sitting trot

Your instructor will sometimes tell you to do a sitting trot. Your bottom should stay in contact with the saddle all the time, not bump out. You need good balance for this, and must relax the lower part of your back so it follows and absorbs the pony's movement.

Diagonals

When you rise to the trot, you rise on one diagonal movement and sit on the other. To do this always on the same diagonal is bad for the pony. You should be aware of which diagonal you are on so that you can change it. When you are trotting in a circle, you should rise as the inside forefoot and outside hindfoot hit the ground. To change the diagonal, sit for an extra beat and then rise again. You should remember to rise on different diagonals, even when you are just going out for a ride.

Lessons in cantering

The canter is a three-beat pace. First the left hindfoot hits the ground, then the left forefoot and right hindfoot together, then the right forefoot. There is a moment between strides when the pony has no feet on the ground. When a pony uses her legs in this order, she is said to be on the right leg because her right foreleg and right hindleg are leading.

Trot to canter
Do a few strides of sitting trot before asking your pony to canter. Stay relaxed as she begins.

Canter to trot
When your pony begins to trot, try not to let her go too fast in the first few strides.

Canter on

A pony can lead with either leg. If you are cantering round a riding school, you should ask your pony to lead with the inside leg. She will then find it easier to canter round the corners. If she leads with the outside leg, it is usually described as being on the wrong leg.

Transitions

To ask your pony to canter on the right leg, put your left leg behind the girth and your right leg on the girth, and squeeze. Feel the right rein, and move your right hip slightly forwards. To change down to trot, sit down in the saddle and feel the left rein.

1 Do not look down to see which leg you are on. Instead, learn to feel which of your pony's shoulders is slightly in front of the other.

2 Sit down to the canter, keeping your bottom in contact with the saddle all the time. Relax your lower back so that your body absorbs the pony's movement.

3 When sitting to a canter on the right rein, your right shoulder and right hip should be slightly in front of your left shoulder and hip.

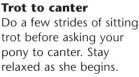

Cantering disunitcd

When a pony leads with one foreleg and the opposite hindleg she is said to be 'cantering disunited'. This can happen if she is unbalanced when she changes direction, and she changes legs either in front or behind. A disunited canter is uncomfortable for both pony and rider.

Perfect canter

The canter should be a lovely, comfortable pace to sit to. Keep your pony balanced so that she takes even strides and canters in a good rhythm. If she becomes unbalanced, you should adjust her speed and energy by gently using your outside rein and inside leg.

Group lessons

Group lessons are a good way to learn to control your pony when he is with other ponies. Always leave a pony's length between your pony and the one in front. If you get too close, your pony may get kicked.

Group words

If you are riding at the front of the group, you are 'leading file'. Your instructor may tell you to trot to the back of the ride. If everyone is to trot, the instructor will say, "Whole ride trot."

School lessons

When you have a riding lesson, it could be in an indoor or an outdoor school, alone with your instructor or in a group. You can learn a lot during lessons, not only from what you do yourself but from what you see other riders doing. As you learn how to control your pony in the riding school, you will gradually gain in confidence.

Changing the rein

In a lesson, you will ride in both directions round the school. When you change direction, it is called 'changing the rein'. You can do this in several ways, such as by riding across the diagonal.

In the school

Points in a school and a dressage arena are marked with a letter. International-sized arenas have extra letters. You need to learn the standard letters because your instructor will give you specific movements to do in the school.

C
H   M
E   B 40m
K   F
A
← 20m →

To remember the standard letters, use a phrase like 'All King Edward's Horses Can Make Big Fences'.

A figure-of-eight is made up of two equal circles. Riding a figure-of-eight involves two changes of rein.

The diagonal goes between two corners, for example F to H. F to E is known as a short diagonal.

Serpentine loops go from one side of the school to the other. All the loops must be the same size.

A 5m loop is a curve of a maximum of 5m in from the long side of the school towards the centre.

Circles can be ridden at several points in the school. You may be asked to ride a 10m, 15m or 20m circle.

Practise on your own

There is a lot to think about when you are having a lesson. You must listen to the instructor and concentrate on controlling your pony. If you can, practise what you have been taught between lessons.

One-to-one lessons

These are the best lessons to have when you are first learning to ride. The instructor can give you all of his or her attention, and you can concentrate fully on the particular thing you are trying to learn.

Working individually

If your instructor asks all the riders in your lesson to carry out different exercises at the same time, you may have to ride past another pony. Ride 'left hand to left hand' past a pony going in the opposite direction.

Lessons on the lunge

Having a lesson on a lunge line is a good
way to improve your seat in the saddle. The
instructor uses a lunge rein and a long whip
to control the pony for you, leaving you free
to concentrate on your riding position.

No reins

Although you will feel
insecure at first, riding
without reins teaches
you how to balance in
the saddle. This means
you will be less likely to
pull on the reins and
hurt your pony's mouth
when things go wrong.

No stirrups

Riding without stirrups
is a good way of
learning how to sit
to the trot. Cross the
stirrups over the pony's
withers so that they do
not hit her sides. Sit
deep in the saddle and
stretch your legs down.

Exercises in the saddle

Doing exercises in the school on your
pony is fun, and it will help to keep
you supple. When you have done the
exercises a few times, you will be a much
more confident rider. To begin with, do not
do any exercises on your own. Wait until an
instructor is present to hold the pony.

Lungeing cavesson

Lungeing is a good way of exercising a pony if you cannot ride her, or if you want to use up some of her energy before you do so. You can ask her to walk, trot and canter on both reins.

For lungeing, a pony wears a special headcollar called a lungeing cavesson. The lunge rein is fixed to a swivel ring on the front. The swivel prevents the rein from tangling as the pony circles around you.

Pony in a lungeing cavesson

Stretching upwards
Hold your arms above your head and stretch up as high as you can.

Stretching forwards
Lean forwards along your pony's neck. Keep your head to one side.

Stretching exercises

There are many different stretching exercises you can do. The best time to do them is before a lesson to warm up your muscles. You can stretch upwards and forwards, backwards to lie on the pony's rump, or down to touch your opposite foot.

Round the world

This is always great fun to do. First, swing your right leg over the pony's neck, so you are facing the side. Then, swing your left leg over her rump so you are facing her tail. Next, swing your right leg over her rump, so you are facing the opposite side. Finally, swing your left leg over her neck so you are sitting facing the front again.

Ankle stretch

With your stirrups crossed and your legs hanging down loosely, point your toes down towards the ground as far as you can, then point them upwards. Point them to the right and to the left, without turning your legs.

Leading rein

When you go out on your first ride, you may go on a leading rein in case you cannot manage your pony out in the open. An experienced rider will hold a long rein attached to your pony's bit. She will have overall control of your pony.

Going out for a ride

Once you have learned to ride, it is fun to go out for a ride, or hack, in the countryside with friends. You will have to cope with all kinds of situations, and you may find your pony behaves differently. If you are still a beginner, you must be accompanied by a responsible adult or your instructor. Even if you are an experienced rider, always tell someone where you are going and at what time you expect to return.

Opening a gate

If the catch on a gate is easy to operate, you can open it without dismounting. Ride your pony right up to the gate so that you can reach out and operate the catch. Push the gate open and, if possible, hold on to it while you walk through. Take care not to let it swing back and hit your pony. Once through, you must close the gate.

Bridle path

You are allowed to ride on special tracks called bridle paths. If a bridle path goes along the edge of a field you must keep to it. You may be able to have a canter if there are no animals in the field.

Through water

If you have to cross a stream or a flooded field, let your pony take his time. Ponies are reluctant to go through water until they know there is a firm base on which to walk.

Coming home

You can enjoy cantering and trotting on your ride, but always walk for the last ten minutes on the way home to let your pony cool down. Never bring a pony back to his stable hot and sweating, because he could catch a chill.

After the ride

When you get home on a hot day, sponge down your pony where he has sweated under the saddle, then walk him around until he is dry. Otherwise, brush the saddle patch, brush off any mud, and check his legs for thorns and scratches.

Riding on the road

Never ride out on your own on the road unless you are sure you can control your pony in any situation. Avoid narrow roads without grass verges and keep off main roads if possible. Learn the proper hand signals and study the rules of the road – they apply to you as well as to drivers. Be polite to road-users and thank drivers who slow down or stop for you – they are then more likely to do so for other riders.

Reflective safety wear

Do not ride on the road at night. If you have to ride on gloomy winter days when the light is poor, wear clothes that reflect car headlights. You can get a hat cover, tabard and belt for yourself, and an exercise sheet, tail guard, bridle cover and leg bands for your pony. You can even get lights to fix to your stirrups.

Asking drivers to slow down
If your pony or the one behind you is nervous of traffic, do not be afraid to ask a driver to slow down, especially if it is a large or noisy vehicle. Hold your outside arm out to the side and move it up and down slowly in a wide arc.

Hand signals

Make signals clearly and in plenty of time. Hold your reins firmly in the other hand so that you keep control of your pony. When you are riding in a group, keep together so that you do not hold up traffic unnecessarily. The rider at the front and back of a single file should make the hand signals. If you are riding in pairs, the riders on the inside of the turn should signal.

Turning right
To tell drivers that you want to turn right, hold your right arm out straight. Check that it is safe before you turn.

Stop
To ask traffic to stop, hold up your right hand high in front of you.

Turning left
To tell drivers that you want to turn left, hold out your left arm. Keep it straight so that your intentions are clear.

Thank you
To say 'thank you' to a driver, raise your hand and smile. If you need to keep both hands on the reins, nod your head clearly so that the driver sees.

Schooling steps

Once you have learned to control your pony and are confident doing basic work in the school, you may progress to more advanced schooling and simple dressage movements. Even if you do not go on to enter any competitions, careful schooling will help you to learn to communicate with your horse or pony and get the most from him.

On the bit

When your pony is working properly it is said to be 'on the bit'. The pony will hold its head vertically, with the mouth lower than your hands. With your pony in this position, you will have maximum control with only a light feel on the reins.

Square halt

With practice, a rider can stop a horse so that he is standing square. This means his forefeet and hindfeet are in line with each other. He must stay in balance throughout the halt.

Turning on the forehand

The horse's hindlegs move round his inside foreleg. To turn to the right, feel the right rein, bring the left rein over in support, press with your left leg and hold the quarters steady with your right leg.

Shoulder-in
The horse's forelegs follow an inner track. He crosses his forelegs as he travels but his hindlegs move straight forwards.

Lateral work

Lateral means 'sideways'. In lateral work, the horse's body forms a curve, so his forelegs move on a different track from his hindlegs. For this reason, lateral work is also known as 'work on two tracks'.

Travers
The horse's hindlegs follow an inner track. His body is bent to the outside of the school.

Leg yield
The horse moves forwards and sideways away from his rider's leg. His body is straight.

Riding side-saddle

To ride side-saddle, you face the front, with your right leg over a pommel called the 'fixed head'. Your left leg rests under another pommel – the leaping head. It is supported by a single stirrup. The saddle is secured by a girth and a balance strap. A pony has special training to carry a side-saddle, and responds to a whip on the right side instead of the rider's leg.

Counter canter

Horses and ponies normally lead with their inside leg when they canter, but for a movement called the counter canter, they need to lead with their outside leg. This is difficult to perform, and the horse needs to be well balanced.

Advanced riding

If you watch a top-class dressage partnership, the horse seems to carry out perfect movements effortlessly, and the rider appears to give no visible aids. It will be a long time before you can carry out advanced dressage paces and movements properly. But remember, even the best riders were not born champions. They have spent many years working hard and patiently.

The art of riding

The classical art of riding is practised by the Spanish Riding School of Vienna in Austria and the Cadre Noir of Saumur in France. Riders at these schools perform complicated steps based on the horse's natural movements. This horse is performing a levade – a controlled half-rear.

Spanish School

Turn on the haunches

This is when a horse pivots round his inside hindleg, which should remain still. He uses his other legs in the same sequence as he would when going forwards.

Collection and extension

Collection is a shortening of the horse's outline. His stride is shorter and more elevated, and the pace is slower. Extension is the opposite. The horse stretches out his head and neck, and he takes longer, lower strides, which increase his speed.

Collected to extended walk
As the horse moves from a collected walk, through medium walk into an extended walk, he gradually lengthens his stride and stretches out his head and neck.

Collected walk

Collected trot
The horse moves at a steady, collected pace, but still with energy. His head and neck are raised and his hindquarters appear lower.

Extended trot
Here, the horse is moving faster, with a longer stride. As he extends the trot, he flicks his front feet forwards.

Flying change

When a horse changes the leading leg at canter, while all his feet are off the ground, it is called a 'flying change'. It is a difficult movement to perform. An experienced horse and rider may do a flying change every stride.

Half-pass

This is a lateral movement in which the horse moves forwards and sideways at the same time. He crosses his outside legs over in front of the inside legs, bending his head in the direction in which he is going. This horse (right) is moving to the left.

In the air
This horse has changed legs in the air, and is now leading with his right leg.

Collected/medium walk

Medium walk

Extended walk

Free walk on a long rein

Collected canter
The collected canter is a slow, rocking pace. The horse must be supple and relaxed. The rider should sit deep in the saddle and follow the movement.

Extended canter
The horse stretches his neck and lengthens his stride to cover as much ground as possible. Both horse and rider's centres of gravity move forwards.

Riding at top speed

Galloping is very exciting for both pony and rider. Do not attempt it until you are sure you can control your pony in canter. Choose a good place to gallop. A smooth field with an uphill slope is ideal – it is easier to stop when going uphill! Never gallop over rough ground, near or up to other ponies, or in a confined space. Make sure there is plenty of room to manoeuvre.

Forward position

When you gallop you should go into 'forward position'. This means leaning forwards and taking your weight on your knees and feet. Raise your bottom just clear of the saddle, but keep in balance. Practise the position first in halt.

Asking for gallop

Get your pony into a good canter and take up the forward position. Urge her forwards with your legs until you are going fast enough for the canter to become a gallop. Keep contact with her mouth through the reins.

The gallop

The gallop is the fastest pace. It is a four-beat pace, with each foot hitting the ground separately. When the left foreleg is leading, the sequence is right hind, left hind, right fore and left fore.

Slowing down

Ponies love to gallop, and they can be difficult to stop. When you want to slow down to canter, maintain contact with your legs and take an upright position again. Resist the forward movement with the reins until the pony responds.

Body position
When you are in forward position, keep your head up and look where you are going.

Suspension
There is a moment in gallop when all four feet are off the ground.

Fast forward

The average pony probably gallops at about 24km/h. This may not sound very fast, but when you are thundering along with the wind whistling past your ears, it certainly feels it! The Thoroughbred is the fastest horse in the world. It gallops at about 50km/h, but its record race speed is an amazing 69.2km/h over 0.4km.

Trotting over poles

When you walk or trot over poles on the ground, it teaches you and your pony to develop balance and rhythm. It shows you both how to approach an obstacle with confidence, and helps you to judge distances.

Keep your head up and look ahead.

Let the pony stretch her neck forwards.

Your pony should take even strides ...

... and tuck up her legs over the poles.

First lessons in jumping

Once you have learned to ride, and have a good secure seat in the saddle, you can start learning how to jump. There are five stages to a jump – approach, take-off, suspension in the air, landing and get-away. As a pony jumps, she stretches her head and neck forwards. You must take up a forward position and go with her.

Between the wings

Trot between the wings of a jump with no pole in place, just to get the feel of it. Go into forward position as you do so. You may find it easier to stay in balance if you shorten your stirrups. Ride through again with a pole on the ground between the wings.

Jumping tips

Always ride your pony forwards with confidence, do not hesitate. If you are unsure, your pony will be worried.

Plan your approach carefully so that you meet the fence straight on.

Do not panic if things go wrong. Ask yourself what it was you did wrong, and try to do better next time.
A refusal

First jump

When you jump, keep a contact with your reins, lean forwards as you take off and do not look down. Return to the saddle as you land. Try to keep your heels down. Hold on to the mane or a neck strap if you need to, so that you do not jab your pony in the mouth.

Getting larger

Once you are confident jumping a low rail, you can try something a bit more ambitious. Keeping fences quite low, but making them wider is a good way to progress. Your pony will have to stretch out further to clear them.

Top-class jumping

To clear huge fences like this (right), the horse has to stretch his head and neck right out. Only a few horses and riders reach this top level. This is Sheila Burke on Genius 79 in the USA in 1998.

Jumping higher

If you want to do really well at showjumping, you need to spend a lot of time schooling your pony. You will need to train on the flat as well as practise over fences. Flat work is important because to jump well your pony needs to be supple and obedient. He must listen to your commands so he does not rush his fences or take off at the wrong moment. When you are jumping, whether for practice or in the ring, you should drive your pony forwards with your seat and legs so that he knows for certain what you want from him.

Seeing a stride

Three or four strides before a fence, try to judge how many strides your pony should take before he takes off. This is called 'seeing a stride'. If a pony gets too near a fence, he will not be able to jump it. If he is too far away, he may knock a pole with his hindlegs.

Water jump

Maria Gretzer (above) rides Feliciano over a water jump at Hickstead, England in 1999. A water jump is a wide pool with a low fence on the take-off side. The horse has to stretch out to jump the obstacle without putting a foot in the water.

Double combination

Four-fence combination

Combination

Two or more fences close together count as one obstacle, called a combination. If a horse refuses at one part, he has to jump the whole sequence again. The number of strides between fences in a combination can vary.

Keeping your own pony

Keeping and looking after your own pony is a huge responsibility. First you must learn how to care for him properly. If he is stabled, you will need to put in hours of hard work every day. If he lives out in a field, you must attend to him each day in all kinds of weather. It's a real commitment – but you'll have a lot of fun too.

Put your pony first
No matter how tired or hungry you are when you come back from a ride, you must always see to the pony's needs first.

Heavy chores
Much of the work of looking after a pony involves lifting heavy objects like buckets of water, and bales of hay and bedding. Learn how to lift things properly, so you do not injure yourself.

The perfect field

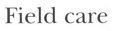

Many ponies live out in fields all the time, and others for some of the time. It is more natural for them than living in a stable, and less work for you. But they cannot live in any old field. It must be properly fenced, have a water supply, and be free of hazards such as barbed wire. You should clear it of poisonous plants, and there should be shade from the sun, and shelter from wind and rain.

Field care

Fields grazed by horses and ponies need good management. They need to be mowed, or topped, to get rid of weeds like thistles and long, rank grass. Then they should be harrowed to aerate the soil, and rolled in spring to level the ground. Ideally, they should also be grazed by cattle or sheep.

Water and fencing

Post and rail is the ideal fencing for horses, but it is expensive. Sagging barbed-wire fences are especially dangerous, and can cause horrific injuries. A self-filling water trough saves a lot of work, but must be cleaned out regularly to get rid of algae.

Living out

In the wild, horses and ponies can travel to find food. In a field, they can eat only what is there. If there are too many ponies in a field they will not get enough to eat. There should be about one horse or two ponies per half hectare of good grazing.

A field shelter

A shelter built facing away from the wind keeps off the worst of the weather. The ponies may also use it in hot weather to get away from flies. Ponies will enjoy licking a mineral block attached to a post.

Picking up droppings

It is important to clean the droppings out of the field regularly, especially if it is not very large and is grazed by lots of ponies. Not only do piles of droppings kill the grass, but if they are left lying around they encourage parasitic worms to breed.

Poisonous plants

Many plants are poisonous if eaten in large quantities; a few are deadly even in small amounts. One of the most dangerous plants that you are likely to find in fields is ragwort. It is tall with ragged leaves and small, yellow, daisy-like flowers. It is very dangerous, whether fresh or dried, and you should pull it up and destroy it. Sprinkle salt on the remains of its roots in the ground to kill them too.

Rhododendron can be deadly to animals

Ragwort should be pulled up and burnt

Yew is deadly, even in small amounts

Foxgloves can be deadly but are not often eaten

Buttercups are mildly poisonous but safe in hay

Acorns in large amounts are poisonous

Hemlock contains a deadly poison

Bracken is very poisonous, but ponies like it

Horsetail is poisonous fresh or dried in hay

Laburnum is highly poisonous

Laurel contains cyanide and can be deadly

Caring for a pony at grass

1 Approach the pony at an angle from the front, holding out a titbit in your hand so he can see it.

2 While he eats the titbit, slip the headcollar rope round his neck in case he tries to move away from you.

3 Put the headcollar over his nose and bring the headpiece round to buckle it on the near side.

4 With one hand near his head and the other at the end of the rope, lead the pony in, looking straight ahead.

Catching a pony

Some ponies are easier to catch than others. If yours is difficult, visit him with a titbit, whether you are going to catch him or not. Never chase him round the field. Wait for him to come to you.

Turning a pony out

Lead the pony through the field gate and close it behind you. Take him right into the field before removing his headcollar. Do this quietly and give him a pat before walking away. Do not wave your arms about to make him gallop off.

You need to visit a pony out at grass every day. Even if you are not going to ride or feed him, you should check that he is all right at least once, and preferably twice, a day. In winter you must check his rug. You may need to take it off and put it on again to make him comfortable. Walk round the field to check the fencing. Make sure the gate is shut and that there is nothing dangerous on the ground.

Breaking the ice

In cold weather, you may need to break the ice on the water trough several times a day. It is useful to keep a stone by it to use for this. Add some warm water to the trough to prevent it from freezing quite as quickly.

Feeding in winter

In winter, there is not so much grass available to eat. Ponies living out will need hay and possibly some hard feed to supplement the grass. The amount will depend on how much work they do, their age and their condition.

Having fun

Ponies do not mind the cold, and it can make them very lively. But they do not like rain and wind. A clipped pony must wear a waterproof rug to keep him warm and dry. Most outdoor rugs have secure fastenings and allow ponies to move freely.

Good stable management

I f you decide to keep your pony in a stable, you need to make sure it is suitable for him. About 3m x 3m is large enough for most ponies, but horses require more space. Purpose-built stables made of brick, wood or breezeblocks are best, but all kinds of buildings can be turned into stables. The stable door should be in two parts so that the top part can be left open. Horses and ponies like to look out over the door and watch what is going on around them. A busy yard keeps them entertained when they are stabled.

Stable toys

Horses and ponies kept in stables for long periods of time can become bored. You can get special toys such as a ball to keep them entertained. Attach a titbit or salt lick to the string, or smear the ball with black treacle.

Stable routine

You will need to visit a stabled pony several times a day. He must be fed, given hay, watered and mucked out – even if you are not going to ride him. He should also spend some time in the field each day. All these things take up a lot of time, and have to be fitted around other commitments, such as school, homework and family life. Work out a realistic routine that you will be able to follow. Ponies are happier when things happen at the same time every day.

Find someone to help you look after and exercise your pony. Sharing a pony can work well if you have a proper agreement as to who is going to do what and when. You can share the expenses too.

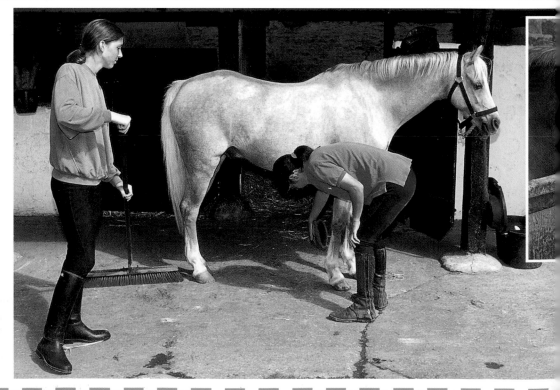

American barn
You may see one of these at your local stables. It is a large barn with loose boxes on both sides of a wide, central aisle.

Loose box
A horse must have plenty of room to lie down. The floor of the box must be non-slip.

Ventilation
Windows must be protected by grilles. They should open inwards to allow air in, but keep rain out.

The ideal stable

The ideal stable is light and well ventilated. It must be waterproof and draught-free, but with good air circulation. It is best situated where the pony can see people and other animals coming and going.

Fixtures and fittings

There are all sorts of fittings that you can put in a stable to make life easier for you and your pony. You may consider giving him a manger to eat his food from, a hay-rack and an automatic watering system. If he likes biting the wood at the top of the door, put on an anti-chew strip.

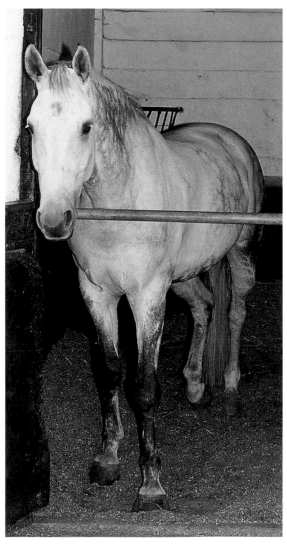

Door hook
Use a hook on the wall to hold open the top of the stable door.

Safety light
A light should be covered and fixed high up, out of your pony's reach.

Stable bolt
This locks on the outside so that your pony cannot open the door.

Kick bolt
This is fixed at the bottom of the door. You operate it with your foot, which is useful if your hands are full.

Horses and ponies have efficient built-in clocks, and know very well when their next meal is due. Work out a timetable for feeding, and try to stick to it at all times – weekends and holidays included.

Door bar
When you can keep an eye on the pony, a bar across the door frame will be enough to keep him in. Most ponies do not try to duck underneath.

Mucking out

You must keep your pony's stable clean. This means frequently removing the droppings – 'skipping out' – and cleaning the stable thoroughly – 'mucking out'. If your pony comes in for just a short time in the day, you can leave the floor bare after mucking out, but you must put down the bed if she is in at night. Some people use a 'deep-litter system' to save time and bedding. They leave the wet bedding for a week or more, and only take out the droppings.

How to muck out

When you muck out a stable thoroughly, you remove all the wet bedding from underneath, as well as the droppings. It is best to do this when the pony is out of the stable. You can leave the floor to dry for a while before replacing the bedding.

Mucking-out equipment

The basic things you need to muck out a stable are a bucket or skip for collecting droppings, a broom, a shovel, a fork and a wheelbarrow. Different forks are made for different bedding. You can use a four-pronged fork or a pitchfork for straw. A shavings fork has lots of prongs.

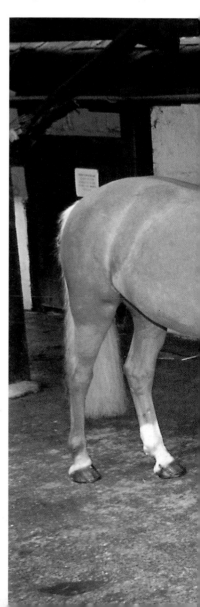

1 First pick up any droppings you can see. Then, using a fork, pile all the clean straw against the walls. You will re-use it later.

2 Use a fork to pick up the wet straw and any droppings mixed in with it. Put the wet straw in a wheelbarrow to take to the muck-heap.

3 Sweep the floor with a stiff broom to clean up any remaining dirt and bits of straw. Shovel these into the wheelbarrow too.

Straw
Straw is comfortable, but ponies often eat it. Some ponies are allergic to the fungal spores in straw, and it makes them cough.

Rubber
This can be used for ponies with a dust allergy, but is not very comfortable. A thin layer of shavings can be put on top.

Shavings
These are more expensive than straw, but they are good for ponies who are allergic to straw. They take time to rot down.

Types of bedding

A pony needs bedding in her stable so that she can lie down and rest. The bedding also stops her from jarring her feet on the hard floor. There are several different types of bedding. You should choose the one that suits your pony.

Shredded paper
This is made from old newspapers and provides a warm, dust-free bed. It is cheap, but it becomes soggy and difficult to handle when it is wet.

4 Wheel the barrow to the muck-heap for emptying. Keep the muck-heap stacked tidily. It will rot down better.

5 Put back the clean straw and add new straw on top. Leave banks of straw around the walls.

Feeding a healthy diet

Ponies naturally feed on grass, and they need to eat a lot of it to gain enough nourishment. If you ask your pony to work, you may need to give him extra hay and other foods called 'hard feed', so he has enough energy. But be careful. Too much hard feed can make a pony ill or unmanageable.

Dried sugar beet – must be soaked before feeding   Bran – high in fibre   Coarse mix – well balanced   Packaged grass – dust free

Soaked sugar beet – ready to eat   Micronized barley – easily digested   Pony nuts – easy to feed   Chaff (chopped straw) – mixed with other feed

Roots and fruits

Ponies love apples, and root vegetables such as swedes and carrots. These are a great treat, but they must be cut up in the right way so that your pony does not choke. Apples and swedes should be cut into slices, and carrots sliced lengthways.

Different feeds

You can mix your own ingredients to make a balanced diet, but coarse mixes and pony nuts are easiest because they are complete, balanced feeds in themselves. Never feed your pony grass cuttings, because they are likely to give him severe stomach pains called colic.

Feeding titbits

All ponies enjoy titbits such as apples, carrots, mints and the 'treats' that you can buy in saddlers' shops and feed merchants. Try to give titbits only as a reward for being good. If you feed too many, some ponies will expect them all the time and may nip you as you walk past.

Rules of feeding

Feed little and often, never just one huge bucket of food. A pony has only a small stomach.

Give your pony mostly bulky, fibrous food, such as grass or hay. This is called roughage.

Match the amount of food you give a pony with the amount of work he is doing.

Make sure your pony has clean fresh water available at all times.

Never feed old or musty food, or hay that has gone mouldy.

Feed your pony at regular times, and keep his bowls clean.

Never guess how much food to give a pony. Weigh it.

Do not feed your pony straight before or after it has done work.

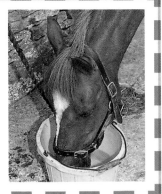

Soaking a haynet

Some ponies are allergic to the dust and fungal spores in hay. They give the ponies a kind of asthma, and make them cough. This affects their performance, making fast work impossible. To remove some of the dust and spores, you can soak hay in a tub of water – a plastic dustbin works well. Allow the hay to drain before feeding it.

Hanging a haynet

A good way to feed hay is in a haynet, rather than loose on the ground. It stops your pony from trampling on the hay and wasting it. Weigh the full haynet so that you know how much you are giving. Hang the net high enough to stop your pony from getting a foot stuck in it, but not so high that hay and seeds will fall in his eyes.

1 Before you start to fill a haynet, open the the top fully to make it easier to push the hay in. Ask a friend to help, or you can use a foot to keep the net open.

2 To hang up the net, pull the string through the ring on the stable wall. A haynet can be quite heavy, so support it from underneath.

3 Pass the string through the bottom of the net, then pull up the net as high as you can. Tie a quick-release knot around the string to secure it.

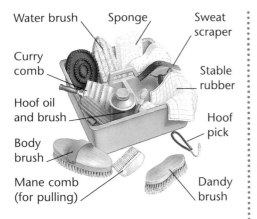

Water brush Sponge Sweat scraper
Curry comb
Hoof oil and brush
Stable rubber
Hoof pick
Body brush
Mane comb (for pulling)
Dandy brush

Grooming kit

There are many different pieces of grooming kit that you can buy, but you only need a few basic items, each designed for a specific job. Keep them in a box and only use them on one pony. A shared kit can spread skin diseases.

Grooming and washing

You should groom a stabled pony every day. This is called 'strapping'. It is hard work, but it will help to tone your pony's muscles as well as keep his skin and coat clean. If your pony lives out, he will need less grooming. Just brush off the dried mud, tidy his mane and tail, and pick out his feet before you ride. Do not remove the grease from his coat because this keeps it waterproof and the pony warm.

1 Clean mud and dirty bedding from the feet with a hoof pick. Work from heel to toe, holding the foot up with one hand.

2 Brush the mane with the body brush, undoing tangles with your fingers. Work down the neck, a small section at a time.

3 Use the body brush with firm, circular strokes all over the pony's body. Clean the brush on the metal curry comb.

Grooming your pony

You should groom your pony properly after exercise, when he is warm and his skin pores are open. Use a dandy brush, or a rubber or plastic curry comb, to remove dried mud. Then clean his coat and skin of sweat and grease with a body brush.

4 Tidy the tail using the body brush and your fingers. Stand to the side, hold the tail in one hand and brush out the hair in sections.

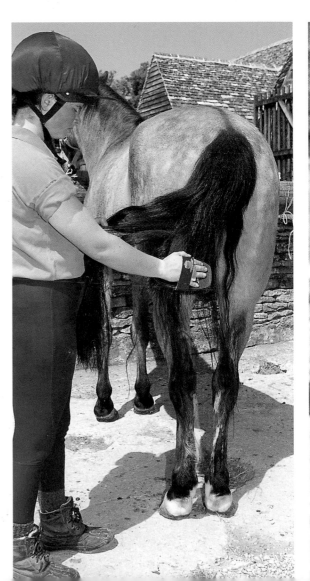

Washing your pony

Give your pony a bath only on a warm sunny day, so he does not get a chill. If the weather is not good, but you want to make him look smart, you can wash his mane and tail and any white socks. Take great care to keep shampoo out of his eyes, and make sure you rinse the soap out thoroughly.

Washing the tail
Use a bucket of water to wash the tail. Lift the bucket, so you get in as much tail as possible. Wet the tail, shampoo it, then rinse until it is squeaky clean.

Washing the body
Warm water from a bucket gets grease out best. Shampoo with a sponge and then rinse. Use a sweat scraper to remove excess water.

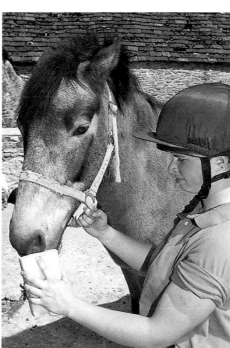

5 To brush your pony's face, take off his headcollar and fasten it round his neck. Brush gently with the body brush.

6 Clean your pony's eyes and nose with a damp sponge. Use a different sponge to wash the dock area under his tail.

Grooming tips

Use the metal curry comb every three strokes so as not to put dirt back on the pony.

Cleaning a body brush

Finish off the mane and tail by 'laying' them down into the correct position with a dampened water brush.

Use a stable rubber to give your pony's coat a final polish. Wipe it over his body in the direction that the coat lies.

Apply hoof oil to make the feet look smart. Put it on clean dry feet with a brush.

Oiling a hoof

Clipping and rugging

In winter, horses and ponies grow longer, thicker coats to keep them warm. If they are then worked hard and fast, they sweat a lot and can lose condition. To avoid this, working horses and ponies have their coats clipped off in a number of different patterns. When clipped horses and ponies are resting, both in the stable and out in the field, they need to wear a rug to compensate for their lack of a warm winter coat.

Bandit clip
The horse is clipped up to his ears, leaving the hair on the front of his face for protection against rain.

Types of clip

A horse may be fully clipped out or just partly clipped. The type of clip chosen depends on the individual horse and the work he is going to do. It is important to remove hair where he is most likely to sweat.

Bib clip
The hair on the head and the front of the neck, chest and shoulders is clipped off. The rest is left.

Blanket clip
A 'blanket' area on the quarters and back, and the legs, is left unclipped. The rest is clipped.

Chaser clip
The line of clipping goes from the ear to the stifle. Steeplechasers are sometimes clipped like this.

Hunter clip
Just the saddle patch and legs are left unclipped to prevent soreness, and to protect against thorns.

Clipping

Your pony must be clean and dry for clipping. The person doing the clip may mark the shape in chalk first. Once a pony has got used to the noise, the clippers are worked against the lie of his coat.

Using a stable rug

1 Put on all types of rug in this way. Fold the rug in half and place it on the pony's back. Put it further forwards than it will finally fit.

2 Unfold the back section of the rug and pull it down over your pony's quarters, smoothing his coat flat as you do so.

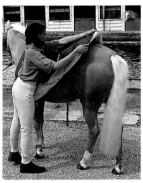

3 Fasten the straps at the front. Check that the rug is in the right position, and not too tight on your pony's shoulders.

4 When you are satisfied that the rug is comfortable, fix the surcingles (crossed straps) or roller under his belly, then the leg straps if there are any.

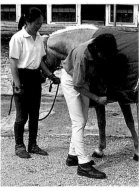

New Zealand rug
This outdoor, winter rug is waterproof and has a warm lining.

Summer sheet
This light rug keeps a horse clean and keeps off the flies. It is useful for travelling to summer shows.

Sweat sheet
This is a kind of string vest that is put on a hot, sweating horse to help him dry off without becoming chilled.

Types of rug

There are many different types of rug and each is designed for a different purpose. Some are for keeping ponies warm and dry, while others are for keeping them clean. They may be made from wool, jute or nylon.

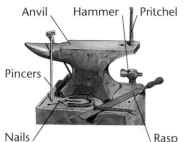

Anvil   Hammer   Pritchel

Pincers

Nails   Rasp

A farrier's tools

These are some of the tools a farrier uses. He hammers red-hot shoes into shape on an anvil and carries them on a spike called a pritchel.

Stamped plain shoe   Fullered shoe   Light racing shoe

Hole for a stud, for extra grip

Heavy shoe for draught horse

Types of shoe

Horseshoes are made of iron. There are different kinds for different work, and some horseshoes are used to correct foot problems. Most shoes have a groove, called fullering, for better grip.

Hot shoeing

Shoeing is usually done hot because the shoes can then be altered easily to fit the pony's feet. Once the shoe is on, the farrier finishes off the foot with a rasp and taps the shoe gently into place.

Shoes and shoeing

Horses' and ponies' feet grow all the time, just like fingernails, and need trimming about every six weeks. If a horse is worked on a hard surface like a road, his feet wear down quickly and get sore, so they are shod for protection. Every few weeks, a farrier removes the shoes, trims the feet, and re-shoes a horse. Shoeing does not hurt.

1 The farrier cuts the clenches, or nail ends, on the old shoe, then levers it off with pincers.

2 Then he trims the hoof with a pair of hoof cutters and tidies up the foot with a rasp.

3 The farrier heats a new shoe in the furnace, then shapes it on the anvil.

4 He tries the hot shoe on the foot. When he is satisfied that it fits, he cools it in water.

5 He hammers the nails through the foot to the side, where he twists off the ends.

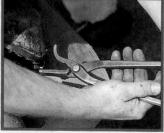

6 He bends down the ends of the nails, to form the clenches which hold on the shoe.

Nailing on the shoe
The farrier hammers the nails through the shoe into the underside of the foot and they emerge at the side.

Protective clothing
A farrier wears a leather apron to protect his legs when he is working.

A farrier's job

It is important for your pony that his feet are shod well, and being a farrier is a skilled job. Most farriers travel to their customers with a mobile, gas-fired forge, in which they heat the shoes. Some farriers do not have a mobile forge, and do cold shoeing – when the shoes are not heated.

Tool box
This box contains all the farrier's tools except the anvil.

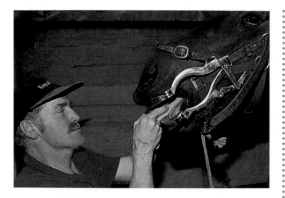

Teeth rasping

A pony's back teeth can wear unevenly, and he may find it hard to chew or get a sore mouth. Ask a horse dentist or vet to check your pony's teeth twice a year. He will use a gag so he does not get bitten, and rasp the teeth smooth.

Your pony's health

A healthy pony has bright eyes, a shiny coat and a good appetite. You should worm and vaccinate him regularly, but there may still be times when he is unwell. He may seem depressed, or be off his food. Or he may have more obvious symptoms, such as lameness, a runny nose or a cough. If you spot any of these signs, ask an experienced adult to help you find out what is wrong. You may need to call the vet.

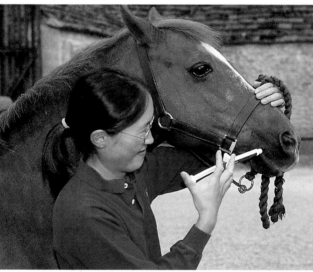

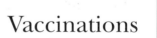

Worming treatments

Grazing horses can easily pick up worms. These live in a horse's intestines and take the nourishment from his food. He will get thin and may die if nothing is done. To prevent this, he must be given regular worm treatments. These can be in the form of a paste squirted on his tongue, or a powder mixed with his food.

Vaccinations

A pony should have a vaccination against equine flu and tetanus every year, because both these diseases can be fatal. A vet will do this for you. It may look painful, but most ponies do not seem to mind it. Keep the record of your pony's vaccinations safe, because you may need to produce it at shows.

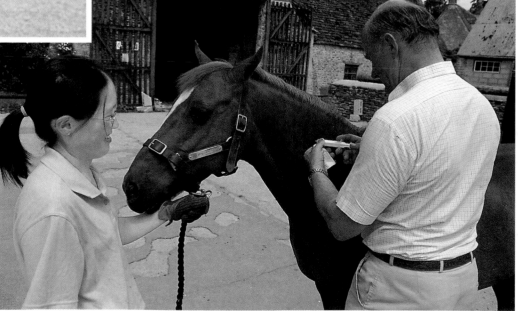

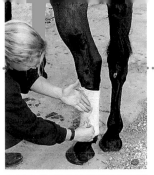

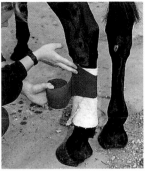

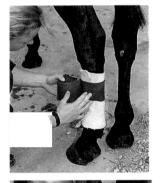

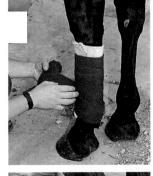

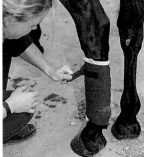

Leg bandages

First wrap a layer of padding such as gamgee round a pony's leg. Start the bandage at the top and work down the leg, overlapping each layer. Keep the padding flat. Make a V-shape with the bandage at the bottom, then work back up. Try to secure the bandage on the outside of the leg. Always bandage both forelegs or both hindlegs, not just one.

Wound powder

Your pony may get small cuts and scratches, especially if he lives out. You can treat these without calling the vet. First wash the wound in clean water, then treat it with an antiseptic spray or powder. This will help the wound to heal, and also keep off flies.

Trotting up
To check for lameness, the vet will ask you to walk and trot the pony on a level, hard surface. The vet will then be able to tell on which leg he is lame.

Calling the vet

If you cannot deal with a problem, call the vet. Never leave your pony for more than 24 hours with a problem no one can explain. Make a careful note of any symptoms so that you can give the vet as much accurate information as possible.

Flexion test
The vet may do a flexion test to check for lameness. This involves bending up a leg tightly and holding it for a few moments before releasing it and immediately trotting the pony. Any lameness will then be obvious.

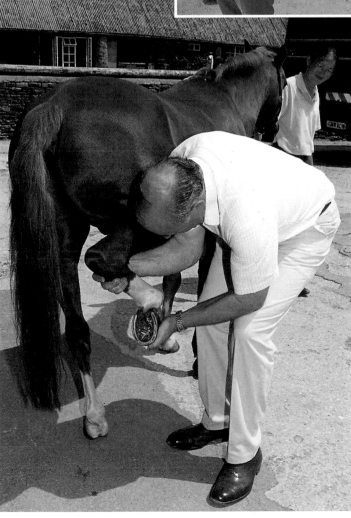

Taking part in events

You may enjoy simply riding your pony around the countryside, but if you want to compete, there are all kinds of activities in which you can take part. You may want to join a riding club or go on sponsored rides. You can enter showing, jumping and gymkhana competitions at local shows, and you might like to try dressage or hunter trials.

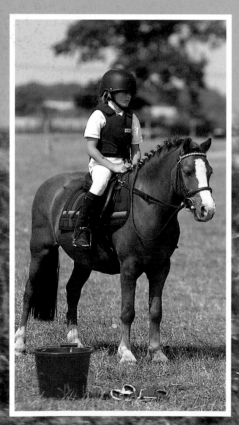

Riding clubs
Local riding clubs hold all sorts of events. If you become a member you can take part, and also find out about other equestrian activities going on in your area.

Endurance riding
If you take part in a long-distance endurance ride, you and your pony will need to be very fit. You may have to cover up to 80km a day. Arab horses have good stamina and excel at this sport.

Vaulting
Vaulting is gymnastics on horseback, and requires great athletic ability as well as riding skills. You can take part on your own or as part of a team, performing leaps and balancing feats with the horse on a lunge rein.

Plaiting the mane

1 Dampen the mane. Start at the top of the neck and divide it into equal bunches. Secure each bunch with an elastic band until you plait it.

2 Plait each bunch tightly and neatly and secure it with an elastic band at the end. Thread a needle with cotton that matches the mane.

3 Tie a large knot in the end of the cotton and sew through the end of the plait. Loop the plait under and sew it firmly in place.

4 Loop the plait in half again and sew it up, catching in any stray hairs. Finish with a knot close to the underside of the plait and cut the cotton.

Getting ready for the show

Getting ready for a show is great fun, but it takes a lot of time and hard work to do it properly. You may need to give your pony a bath, if the weather is warm enough, otherwise you can just groom him thoroughly. You will need to wash his mane and tail before plaiting them. You can also oil his hooves and make sure his tack is really clean so that he will look his best.

Bands or sewn?
You can secure your pony's plaits with elastic bands, but if you are entering a showing class or competing in dressage, you must sew them in place.

Making the most of your pony

Quarter marks

Make quarter marks on your pony's hindquarters by wetting the coat and brushing it at different angles. You can also use special stencils to make squares or diamonds. Use hair spray to make the marks last longer.

Trim hairy fetlocks and any coarse hairs under the jaw.

Make white tails and markings extra white by rubbing in chalk.

Oil the hooves when they are clean, to make them look smart.

Pulling a mane

Pull a mane to tidy it up before you plait it. Use a pulling comb to separate a few long hairs at a time from underneath, then pull.

Hairdressing
If you end up with a few wisps of hair sticking out of the plaits, put some hair gel on them and smooth them down flat.

Plaiting the forelock
Dampen the forelock and plait it in the same way as the mane, sewing it and securing it as before. To make the plait stand out at the top, cross the strands of hair underneath as you are plaiting, instead of over the top.

Trimming
Carefully trim any long hairs in the ears. Fold the sides of the ears together and trim off the hairs that stick out.

Plaiting tips
You should give your pony an even number of plaits, including the forelock. Depending on his size, he may have seven, nine or eleven plaits on his neck. A lot of plaits make a short neck look longer. Fewer, thicker plaits make a long neck look shorter. If you are good at plaiting, you can make the plaits sit up or lie flat to make the neck look wider or narrower.

Baby oil
Wipe a little baby oil or petroleum jelly around the muzzle of a dark-skinned pony to make it look clean and shiny.

Plaiting the tail
Plait an unpulled tail for neatness. Take long hairs from each side of the dock and plait them with hair from the centre. Gradually take in more hair from the sides as you work down the tail. Secure the end, fold it under and sew it in place.

Getting ready to travel

If you compete in shows or riding-club events, you will have to move your pony from place to place in a horsebox or trailer. Most ponies do not mind travelling once they have got used to it. They learn to stand with their legs braced to absorb the movement, and become good at balancing. But they do need to wear special equipment to protect them from accidental knocks and bumps.

Ready to go

This pony has been prepared for a show and is ready to load into a horsebox or trailer. The rug is useful to keep her clean, even in warmer weather.

Bandaging the tail

A bandage keeps the top part of your pony's tail lying flat and neat. It also stops it from rubbing against the back wall of the box or trailer. You can use a tail-guard instead of a bandage, or put one on top of the bandage.

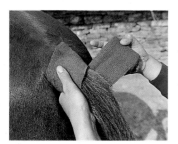   

1 Start to bandage the tail, leaving a corner of the bandage's end sticking out at the top.

2 After a few turns around the tail, fold the end down and wind the bandage over it.

3 Bandage to the end of the dock, then work back up. Tie the strings with a bow.

4 Fold a layer of bandage over the bow to stop it from coming undone.

Removing a tail bandage

To take off a tail bandage, unfold the part over the tie, undo the strings and slide the whole thing off, laying the tail hair flat as you do so. Roll up the bandage again, starting at the tie-strings end with the strings on the inside.

Loading up

Walk your pony confidently up the middle of the ramp. Some ponies will walk straight into a trailer. If your pony is unsure, take a little time, and try lifting one of her front feet on to the ramp. She may prefer it if she can see a light at the front end of the trailer.

Roller
A roller holds the rug in place. A pad underneath stops it from pressing on the pony's spine.

Clean tail
To keep the tail out of the way, put on a tail bandage, then fold up the tail and secure it with an elastic band.

Rug
A rug keeps the pony warm when travelling in cooler weather.

Travel boots
Soft, padded boots protect the legs from accidental injury. Velcro straps make them easy to put on and take off.

Tying up

Tie up your pony in the trailer fairly short so she cannot move her head about too much. Tie the rope to string, using a quick-release knot. Some trailers and horseboxes have a tying-up chain fixed on each side of the horse's head, level with the chin.

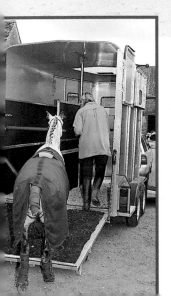

Going to a show

Competing in a show is great fun. After all the preparation, it is exciting to ride round the ring, looking your best and trying your hardest. In between classes, do not tear around, but let your pony rest in the shade. Give him a drink and some hay or grazing. It is great to win a rosette, but do not blame your pony or get upset if you fail to do so. There is always next time.

Unloading backwards
If your pony needs to back out of a trailer, stand at his head and push him gently backwards. Ask someone to stand by the ramp to guide him.

Unloading safely

Untie your pony before you take down the breastbar or rear strap. Lead him out forwards if you can. When you go down the ramp, do not let him rush. Some ramps are slippery and quite steep, and he could hurt himself if he goes too fast. Ask two friends to stand on either side of the ramp if you think he might try to jump off sideways.

Unloading forwards
If the box or trailer has a side ramp, you can lead your pony out forwards. Do not let him pull you out. Walk down calmly.

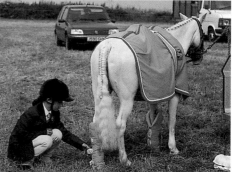

First things first
Tie up your pony or ask someone to hold him while you take off his boots. Check him all over to see that he is all right after the journey.

Ready to jump

If you are entering a jumping event, you must wear a body protector that meets the safety standards.

Ready to show

Look as smart as you can for a showing class. It will give you confidence if you look your best.

Waiting safely

Leave your pony tied to a trailer only if you know he will not get upset. Fasten his lead rope to a piece of string so he can break free if he panics. Your pony will probably wait patiently if you hang up some hay for him.

The secretary

When you arrive at the showground, check in at the show secretary's tent or trailer. You can collect your number here and enter classes if you have not already done so. You can also find the results of classes here. The secretary will post them up on a noticeboard.

Sharing a pony

If you are sharing a pony with a friend, make sure you agree in advance which classes you will enter. It is fun to watch each other and help prepare for the classes. But do not ask your pony to do too much and exhaust him.

Fun and games

At gymkhanas and shows there are all kinds of games and races for you to try. Some are for teams, and some for individuals. You need to be good at games, able to think and act quickly, and to have an obedient and fast-moving pony. If you belong to a pony club you could become a member of the team and compete around the country.

Handy tips

You need to be quick-witted, fit and athletic to do really well in mounted games.

Your pony must be fast, agile, and above all, obedient – it is no use asking him to gallop if you cannot get him to stop or turn.

Practice makes perfect

No matter what games you enter, you need to practise for them. Schooling your pony until he is obedient to all your commands will make a big difference on the day. Practise going from halt to canter to gallop, and changing pace and direction at speed. See how quickly you can mount and dismount, and learn how to vault on and off. You can also get used to leaning out of the saddle to pick up things.

Vaulting on

Being able to vault on to your pony while he is moving saves a lot of time in games and races. It is easier if your pony is small and you have long legs! You have to run with him, holding the saddle, then spring up and swing yourself over.

Flag relay
This is a team game in which you have to gallop to a flag, lean over and pick it up, then gallop back and hand it on to the next member of your team.

Barrel racing
A pony that can gallop and turn quickly without losing his balance is a great help in this race round barrels.

Egg and spoon
You need a steady hand for this. The eggs are not real, but you still have to keep one on the spoon!

Tyre race
You and a partner have to leap off your ponies, climb through a tyre and then get back on again.

Make a tower
You have to lean right out of the saddle to stack the plastic tubs without overbalancing in this race.

Potato race
Having picked up a potato and raced down the field, you then have to throw it into a bucket.

Showjumping classes

Showjumping is a popular riding sport. All classes have a time limit, but some are against the clock, where the fastest clear round wins. You are penalized for knocking down a fence, refusing, running out (going round the side of a fence) and falling. Three refusals or taking the wrong course means elimination. If more than one person jumps a clear round, there is a 'jump off'. This means you have to ride a shorter course to decide the winner.

Walking the course

Before a showjumping class, all the competitors have a chance to walk the course. This gives you time to plan and memorize the route you will take. You can also look carefully at each jump, and judge how many strides your pony will need to take between the parts of the combination fences.

In the collecting ring

The collecting ring is an area, usually with one or two practice jumps, where you can warm up your pony before his class. Once the class has started, you will have to wait near the entrance to the ring for your number to be called.

Triple bars
Three bars making a wide spread

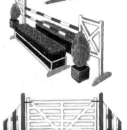

Brush and rails
A spread highest in the centre

Gate
A high, upright fence

Wall
Made of 'bricks' that fall off easily

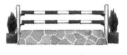

Filler
A solid part below the poles

Upright poles
Poles straight above each other

Double oxer
Brush between two sets of poles

Hog's back
The highest pole is in the centre

Types of jump

Show jumps fall into four main categories: uprights, spreads, combinations and water. Uprights are difficult for ponies to jump. Spread fences are easier because they are lower at the front. Combinations – jumps with only a stride or two between each fence – need good judgment from pony and rider. To clear water jumps, ponies have to stretch themselves out.

Thinking ahead

Throughout your round, it is important to keep a good position in the saddle. Urge your pony forwards confidently as you jump, and look ahead to the next fence.

Saving time

It is important to memorize the course before you enter the ring so that, as you land from each jump, you can be thinking about the next one. Against the clock, you can save precious seconds by taking the shortest route between fences.

Clear round

Do not tear around the ring – your pony will lose balance and hit fences.

Drive him firmly towards each fence. If he feels you hesitate, he is likely to refuse.

If you feel he may refuse, a sharp tap with your stick behind the girth may work.

Do not hit your pony if he knocks a fence – just try to approach it better next time.

Showing and dressage tests

To compete in the show ring and dressage arena you need a well-schooled horse or pony, and both of you must be clean and smart. In the show ring, a pony is judged on his conformation (his shape and proportions), his paces and his behaviour. You will have to ride at walk and trot, and canter on both reins; walk and trot your pony in hand; and sometimes do an individual show.

Showing in hand

When you are lined up in the ring, you will be asked to take off your pony's saddle so that the judge can inspect him. Then you will have to walk and trot him in hand so the judge can check that he moves straight.

Individual show

An individual show is a chance to show off your pony's paces. Most people ride circles at trot and canter on both reins, or combine them to form a figure-of-eight. At the end of your time, finish with a good square halt.

Before the test

Before doing a dressage test, ride in a pony thoroughly to get him settled and working at his best. Some horses and ponies need more work than others, so give yourself plenty of time.

Riding the test

Concentrate and keep calm when riding in the dressage arena. The judges who mark the test write their comments on a score sheet. You will be given the sheet, and it is a useful pointer to your strengths and weaknesses.

Dressage hints and tips

Check that your clothes and tack meet the requirements of the competition.

Make sure that you and your pony are immaculately clean and well-groomed. It is important to make a good first impression on the judges.

Ask someone to call out each bit of the test as you practise, to help you to remember it.

Make up rhymes to help you memorize the test.

Practise until you and your pony can carry out the test's requirements perfectly.

Aim for the top

Some riders and their horses specialize in dressage. Isabell Werth and Nissan Gigolo are doing an extended trot at the World Equestrian Games in 1998. A great deal of training lies behind the tests performed by top-class horses and riders.

Hedge

Ski jump

Log

Tyres

Rails

Cross-country

On a cross-country course, there are solid fences with long spaces in between. Both you and your pony need to be strong and brave. You will pick up penalty points for every mistake you make, such as refusing, jumping the wrong part of a fence, going the wrong way, falling off or going over the time limit. The fences carry red and white flags. You must jump between them with the red on your right and the white on your left. You may have the choice between an easier, slower route or a faster, more difficult one.

Types of fence

Cross-country fences are based on obstacles you might meet if you were riding through the countryside, such as rails, hedges, logs, walls, ditches, banks and water. They are solid and do not give way if hit. They may be placed so that you have to jump them going up, or down, hills.

Hunter trials

Cross-country jumping competitions are called hunter trials. There are trials for both horses and ponies. Courses often take you through fields and woodland, and you may have to open and close a gate. There is usually a set time in which you must try to finish one section or the whole course.

Walking the course

You are allowed to walk round a cross-country course before you ride it. This allows you to look at the fences and work out the best way to approach them. Check the ground on the approach and landing, and look out for things that might spook your pony, so that you are prepared.

Horse trials

In horse trials, you must do dressage, cross-country and showjumping. These are the supreme test of horse and rider. Precision and training is needed for the dressage; speed, endurance and boldness for the cross-country; and suppleness and obedience for the showjumping. Experienced riders take part in events that last for two or three days. This is Andrew Nicholson and New York, at a three-day event.

Steeplechase

Two- and three-day events include a steeplechase phase – about 12 fences over a distance of about 3.6km. The course has to be ridden at around 41km/h, which means a horse has to perform like a racehorse. At large events, competitors also have to ride along sections of roads and tracks, both before and after the steeplechase.

Glossary

Gallop – the fastest gait

Gymkhana game

The horse and pony world has a language of its own, and you might not understand all the words you read and hear. This list explains what some of these words mean.

action The way a horse or pony moves.

aids The signals that a rider uses to tell a horse what to do. Natural aids are the rider's legs, **seat**, hands and voice. Artificial aids include whips and spurs.

bit The part of a bridle that goes in a horse's mouth – usually made of steel.

blaze A white mark down the front of a horse's face.

bounce fence A combination fence with no stride between the two elements. A horse lands from one and immediately takes off again for the other.

breastplate A strap that goes round a horse's neck and fastens to the front of the saddle and to the girth. It prevents the saddle from slipping backwards.

bucking A horse kicking out his back legs, with his head down, or jumping up in the air with all four feet off the ground and his back arched.

cantle The back of a saddle.

cavesson a) A type of noseband. b) A headcollar with swivel rings to which a lunge rein is attached.

changing the rein Changing the direction in which you are riding in the school or show ring.

chaps Leather or suede over-trousers to protect a rider's legs when riding. They may be full-length, or half-chaps up to the knee.

clipping Removing a horse's winter coat so he sweats less when working.

collecting ring A small ring outside the main show ring, where competitors gather before a class.

colt A male horse under the age of four years.

conformation The overall shape and proportions of a horse or pony.

curry comb a) A metal comb on a wooden handle used for cleaning a body brush when grooming. b) A plastic or rubber version that can be used on a horse to remove mud or loose hairs.

diagonal When a horse trots, his legs move in diagonal pairs: near fore and off hind, off fore and near hind. A rider rises on one **stride** and sits on the other, and so is said to be on the right or the left diagonal.

dishing A horse moving by throwing his front feet out to the sides instead of going straight; a fault in his action.

dismount To get off a horse or pony.

disunited Cantering with one leg leading in front and the opposite leg leading behind.

double bridle A bridle with two bits, used mostly for dressage and showing.

dressage The advanced schooling and training of a horse, performed in competitions.

dropped noseband A noseband that fastens under the bit, preventing a horse from opening his mouth to avoid the action of the bit.

extension A lengthening of a horse's **outline**, so he moves faster with longer, lower strides.

feather The long hair that grows around the **fetlocks** of heavy horses and also of some ponies.

fetlocks The joints on the lower part of a horse's legs just above the feet.

filly A female horse under the age of four years.

flat work Schooling 'on the ground', not over fences.

flying change Changing the **leading leg** at canter when a horse has all four feet off the ground.

foal A horse or pony under the age of one year.

forehand The head, neck, shoulders, **withers** and forelegs of a horse or pony.

forelock The part of the mane that hangs between a horse's ears and covers the forehead.

forward position The position in which a rider sits when galloping and jumping – leaning forwards with the seat off the saddle, taking the weight on the knees and feet.

frog The V-shaped structure in the sole of a horse's foot.

gait The manner in which a horse or pony moves. The natural gaits are walk, trot, canter and gallop. Other gaits can be taught (see **pace**).

gamgee Cotton wool lined with gauze, used as padding under leg bandages.

gelding A castrated male horse or pony – i.e. one not able to breed.

girth The broad strap that goes round a horse's belly to hold the saddle in place.

going The condition of the ground for riding: wet ground is described as soft or heavy going; dry ground is described as hard going.

gymkhana Mounted games and races, usually performed as part of a show.

hackamore A type of bitless bridle.

Numnah

Rider in casual turn out

Dapple-grey horse

Shetland pony mare with foal

Riding whips

hands a) The units of measurement used for a horse's height. One hand equals 10cm. b) A rider who has light yet positive control of the reins is said to have good hands.

hard feed Food such as oats, barley, maize, coarse mix and horse nuts, which are fed in small quantities, as opposed to bulk feeds such as grass and hay.

impulsion The energy a rider creates in a horse by the use of the legs and seat.

in hand Leading a horse while on foot.

jump off An extra round or rounds, used to decide the winner in showjumping when two or more competitors have the same score.

leading file The front horse and rider of a group.

leading leg The leg that is in advance of the others in canter.

leg up An easy way of getting on a horse. A helper holds a rider's left leg and helps him or her to spring up into the saddle.

loading Putting a horse into a horsebox or trailer.

loose box A separate stable, in which a horse is free to move around.

lungeing Exercising a horse on a long rein attached to a special headcollar. The horse is asked to walk, trot and canter in circles.

manège An enclosed riding arena.

mare A female horse or pony aged four years or more.

near side The left side of a horse or pony.

neck strap A strap that passes round a horse's neck either a) for a rider to hold on to, or b) part of a martingale or **breastplate**.

novice An inexperienced rider or horse.

numnah A saddle-shaped pad used under a saddle to prevent it from rubbing and to absorb the horse's sweat.

off side The right side of a horse or pony.

outline The shape a horse's or pony's body makes when he is being ridden.

pace a) Another word for **gait**. b) A specific gait in which a horse moves both legs on one side together.

Palomino A horse or pony with a golden coat and a white mane and tail. In some countries, Palominos are recognized as a breed in their own right.

pelham A type of **bit** with two reins and a curb chain.

points a) The visible features of a horse. b) Areas on a horse that are described as part of his colour. A horse with 'black points' has a black mane, tail and lower legs.

pommel The front part of a saddle.

pulling a mane and tail Pulling out a few long hairs to tidy up a mane and tail.

quarter marks Decorative patterns made on the **quarters** by brushing against the lie of the coat with a damp brush.

quarters The area of a horse behind the saddle – his hindquarters and hindlegs.

quick-release knot A knot used to tie up a horse. Pulling the end of the rope releases the knot instantly.

rearing Going up on the hind legs.

roller A broad band that fastens round a horse's belly to hold a rug in place.

schooling Training a horse.

seat a) A rider's position in the saddle. b) The part of the saddle on which a rider sits.

shying Jumping sideways when startled.

skewbald A coat colour with large, irregular patches of brown and white.

skipping out Collecting droppings from a stable in a basket or skip.

sound A sound horse is a healthy one, free from any sign of lameness and breathing problems.

spread fence A wide fence with the back part higher than the front.

stallion A male horse or pony, aged four years or more, used for breeding.

strapping Thorough grooming of a horse, usually done after exercise.

stride The distance travelled by a horse's foot between two successive impacts with the ground.

surcingle a) A strap attached to a rug, used to fasten it round a horse's belly. b) A strap that goes over a racing saddle for extra security.

tack All the pieces of saddlery used on a riding horse or pony.

Thoroughbred The fastest breed of horse.

transition The change from one **pace** to another. An upward transition is from a slower to a faster pace; a downward transition is from a faster to a slower pace.

tree The framework on which a saddle is built.

turn out a) To let a horse loose in a field. b) The appearance of a horse and rider. c) A vehicle pulled by a horse or pony.

vaulting a) Jumping up on to a horse without using the stirrups. b) Gymnastics on horseback.

wind A horse's breathing.

wings The extensions at the sides of a jump.

withers The bony ridge at the base of a horse's neck.

worming Giving medicine to kill parasitic worms inside a horse's intestines.

Index

HORSE AND PONY WEB SITES
www.equiweb.co.uk/centres/talland/index.htm
www.pony-club.org.uk (official Pony Club site)
www.horse-advice.co.uk (healthcare and other advice)
www.ilph.org (International League for the Protection of Horses)
www.horselink.co.uk (links the top horse and pony sites)
www.newrider.com (advice and information for keen new riders)
www.bhs.org.uk (official British Horse Society site)
www.equiworld.net (international horse and pony information)
www.swhp.regd-charity.org.uk (Society for the Welfare of Horses and Ponies)

Kingfisher would like to thank:
The Hutton family and Patricia Curtis, as well as the models: Alison Jane Berman, Parker Dunn, Theo Freyne, Emma Harford, Brian Hutton, Charlie Hutton, Pippa Hutton, Pete Jenkins (equine dentist), Eric Lin, Lucy Miller (advanced riding), Charlotte Nagle, Jay Rathore, Nicola Ridley, Ignacio Romero Torres, Victoria Taylor, Sophie Thomas, Ayako Watanabe and Sawako Yoshii.

Jacket photographs: Only Horses Picture Agency; gettyone Stone/Art Wolfe